Sundays Down South

Sundays Down South

A Pastor's Stories

JAMES O. CHATHAM

University Press of Mississippi • *Jackson*

http://www.upress.state.ms.us

07 06 05 04 03 02 01 00 99   4 3 2 1

∞

Library of Congress Cataloging-in-Publication Data

Chatham, James O., 1937–
   Sundays down South : a pastor's stories / James O. Chatham.
      p.   cm. — (Folklife in the South series)
   ISBN 1-57806-175-X (hardcover : alk. paper).
      1. Southern States—Social life and customs—1865–   Anecdotes.
   2. Southern States Biography Anecdotes.   3. Southern States—Social
   conditions—1945–   Anecdotes.   4. Chatham, James O., 1937–
   Anecdotes.   5. Clergy—Southern States Biography Anecdotes.
   I. Title. II. Series.
   F216.2.C47   1999
   975.04—dc21   99-24148
                                                                       CIP

British Library Cataloging-in-Publication Data available

Cheer up, my brother
    live in the sunshine;
we'll understand it
    all by and by.

—W. B. Stevens, "Farther Along"

CONTENTS

Introduction   ix

Contents

INTRODUCTION

"We may'uv been born poor, but that don't stop us from livin' rich."
Betty Squire, 1967

Life in the South has been an unending struggle.

A struggle for money: except for a few urban centers, the South has essentially lived in perpetual economic depression.

A struggle with direction: we in the South have never fully decided whether we want to move toward the future or toward the past.

A struggle with violence: deep in our nature has been a tendency to respond to problems with force. The tendency has seldom served us well and has usually served us quite poorly.

A struggle with religion: we have been taught through childhood that God and the church need to stand at the center of our lives. And then we have spent our adulthood recovering from religion's rigidity, its exclusiveness, and the deep sense of guilt it has implanted in us.

A struggle with race: black southerners have worked longer and harder than anyone else in building the region, and yet black southerners have not to this day been accorded full human status and dignity.

A struggle with education: we in the South have not ever fully decided whether we think education is a good idea.

A struggle with gender. We have asked women to live a paradox: appearing on the surface to be weak, dependent, and helpless, always catering to the needs and wishes of men, while on the interior being strong, intelligent, determined, and necessarily devious. We have asked men to live a different paradox: appearing on the surface to be strong, dominant, courtly, and chivalrous while hiding the dependence, insecurity, and violence that dwells within them. Neither gender has lived its split personality particularly well.

A struggle with how the rest of the nation views us: as barefoot bumpkins so primitive that we definitely need outside help if we are to accomplish anything significant.

A struggle over people who are different: we have harbored an inbred suspicion and distrust of anyone not like us.

A struggle with the fact, as historian C. Vann Woodward said in *The Burden of Southern History,* that we are the only Americans who have ever lost a war (certainly true until Vietnam). We therefore have borne an inner pathos, a humility, a sense of our own limits that the rest of the nation, in its opinionated self-certainty, has not shared.

A struggle with heat and humidity. Because of warm moisture sucked out of the Gulf of Mexico and spread across the region by the trailing side of advancing high-pressure systems, there is only a brief time in winter when the heat and humidity fully go away.

On the wall of many an old southern home I have seen that painting — I have no idea who painted it — of a Civil War soldier still clad in his military gray. The war is over. The soldier has been defeated. He has traveled the long distance back home with the defeat heavy on his heart. He has arrived at his destination to find his home place burned and destroyed, his kinfolks killed or scattered. Viewing the rubble, which is visible in the background of the painting, the soldier leans on his rifle, pouring forth tears of despair, sobbing uncontrollably over the death of his past, unable for the moment to see any future. But even in this, his darkest hour, he holds himself with an erectness, he bears in his body a pride, a promise to carry him forward. The viewer weeps with him, sharing his deep and painful hurt, but also gets the clear message that, because of his determination and grit, the final chapter of this saga has not yet been written. The painting would not classify as notable art; I have never seen it in a museum. But it expresses the proud and bitter determination of many southern hearts to arise from the ash heap and prove that we can win.

Southerners survive! We make it! We are not defeated by the struggle! We aggregate together in support. We cope. There is an innate determination in us that does not lose its direction. We somehow manage to believe our region's dominant theology: that the defeat of Friday night will be followed by the victory of Sunday morning, no matter how long and dark Friday night may be. Some combination of community, faith, and stubbornness will bear us up.

This book contains stories from the struggle, stories of the experiences of a southern pastor with southern people, stories from thirty years of life in four widely different locations.

Pastors have a unique view into life. We are present with people literally from birth to death. We baptize them, confirm them, marry them, counsel them, and finally bury them. We are confidants. People trust us with a great deal of less-than-public information. We can ask nearly any question we want and almost always get a truthful answer. Part of our task is to reflect with people on the meaning of their lives, to try to interpret what happens, and to find a good way into the future. It is a unique role. No one else has this broad an entrée into the lives of everyday folk. It generates an unending progression of tales that tell who people are and what their lives are made of.

Many of the accounts in this book describe southern culture, the unique ways we in the region have done things. A few tell of people who have fought against the future, trying vainly to maintain what used to be. Most tell of people who, in one way or another, worked their way through the struggle and survived. I count some of these people as true heroes, men and women whose stories need to be told.

I have been a pastor for three decades in four southern locations. I have arranged the stories of this book into four blocks, corresponding to the locations. I was first in Covington, a paper mill town in the mountains of far western Virginia. I worked there while I was a seminary student, during 1962 and 1963. I was next in southwest Mississippi, a pastor in the small town of Fayette, population sixteen hundred, and in the nearby village of Union Church, population probably two hundred, from 1964 to 1966. I worked next in the inner city of Winston-Salem, North Carolina, serving as pastor there from 1966 until 1973. And I have been in Louisville, Kentucky, since 1977.

Different parts of the South are very distinct. The western Virginia mountains bear little resemblance to inner-city Winston-Salem, and neither is very much like southwest Mississippi. And yet all are distinctly southern. I was a pastor in Ohio from 1974 to 1977, and I learned what southern means: less hurried, less rigid, less abrupt, less self-certain, more relational, more "warm," more trusting, more slow, more family-rooted — for better and for worse. All four locations have borne this basic southernness.

Life in four locations has given me a larger perspective that significantly affects this writing. The South cannot be defined by one place. We are many places. Some knowledge of the many creates a different interpretation of the one. I can see Covington more clearly, Fayette more clearly, Winston-Salem more clearly, Louisville more clearly, because I have been immersed in all four.

Numerous pastors have collected stories from their pastoral experiences. Sermons have been full of these tales, and, now and then, story collections have been published. The purpose has usually been devotional reflection, however.

In *The Lord's Boarding House: Vignettes of Pastoral Care* (Nashville: Abingdon Press, 1985), Nico Ter Linden, a Dutch pastor, relates stories from his work in parishes from northern Holland to Kansas to Amsterdam. He designs his stories to stimulate theological reflection on particular subjects: gratitude, "the Lord is my shepherd," doubt, polarization, praying with a neighbor, punishment, dying, and so forth. The culture from which each story comes has little significance within his purpose, reflecting on universal dimensions of the human experience.

Bob Libby, an Episcopalian priest, draws on parish stories from Florida and Georgia as a starter for devotional meditation in *Grace Happens: Stories of Everyday Encounters with Grace* (Cambridge, Mass.: Cowley Publishing, 1994). Again, it matters little where the stories originated.

Michael L. Lindvall, in *The Good News from North Haven: A Year in the Life of a Small Town* (New York: Doubleday, 1991), presents a series of stories from a "fictional" parish in Minnesota to convey, as it were, the story of small-town parish life. It is amusing, it is descriptive of the culture, and it is probably less fictional than the author suggests.

In *Diary of a City Priest* (Kansas City, Mo.: Sheed and Ward, 1993), John P. McNamee recounts tales from his twenty-five years as a priest in a poor area of Philadelphia. His is a highly reflective book, beautifully written, exploring the life of poverty and the heart of the pastor in relation to that life.

Elmer L. Townes tells of his beginning parish, Westminster Presbyterian Church in Columbia, South Carolina, in *Stories about My First Church* (Ventura, Calif.: Regal Books, 1997). His purpose is clearly moralistic. He concludes each story with, "Principles to Take Away," moral guides for living.

None of these volumes parallels my purpose. I seek to tell the stories of particular southern people in their struggles with life, stories witnessed by their pastor. I cannot locate any volume previously written that bears this same purpose.

In telling these stories I have used a number of actual names. I have done so because I think both the people named and their relatives would be proud to have the tales ascribed publicly to them.

Where I have thought a story might reflect at all poorly on someone, I have changed the names well beyond recognition. I have no wish to portray any identifiable person negatively. My purpose is to convey the pictures of what happened.

The stories come primarily from my memory. In a few cases I have researched events to make sure primary facts are in order. I have also talked with a number of the people who were involved. But mostly these tales represent what I saw, heard, and now recall.

And, finally, this is not a religious book. It does not intend to teach, preach, or espouse religion. And yet most southerners are incomprehensible apart from religion.

Traditional wisdom holds that when you meet southerners, you first find out their names, and you next find out where they go to church. Those are the two essential beginnings of southerner identity.

To try to tell the stories of southerners without mentioning religion would be like trying to describe the ocean without mentioning water. A huge, critically significant dimension would be missing. The book is therefore laced with religious references. Biblical language appears often. But the book is not primarily about religion.

I seek to paint cultural pictures of four locations, to tell the tales of both heroism and tragedy, of ingenuity and vanity, of champions and fools, and to show what I have found to be the unending determination of my southern brothers and sisters to "live in the sunshine."

Sundays Down South

Covington, Virginia
1962–1963

Covington was built around a huge paper mill, on the Norfolk and Western rail line in western Virginia, fewer than ten miles from the West Virginia border. The town occupied a valley that winds among several mountains. The mill stacks poured out continuous billows of white ash that saturated the air for miles around. A pungent odor penetrated everything. The smoke left a dirt film even in the most carefully sealed spaces. Local lore advised, "If you hang your clothes on the line, they will get dirty before they get dry." But the corollary wisdom was, "Dirt is money!"

These were the times before the mill owners discovered that they were pouring tons of valuable residue up those stacks and that they could make a sizable profit by scrubbing the smoke. While I was in Covington, cleanup talk was labeled communist subversion.

The mill's managers hid their residences on the far side of a western hill—in which direction the wind seldom blew. But the labor, for the sake of easy access, lived straight up a hillside overlooking the mill. The white ash settled over everything. There was a morning ritual called "sweeping down" in which everyone worked valiantly against impossible odds to try to clean up front porches and sidewalks. At least it made you feel better for a few hours. It was before the days of rampant medical lawsuits, and no one really wanted to know what all that ungodly soot was doing to our lungs.

The church in which I worked was located directly between the labor village and the mill. Several hundred workers passed it each day. I overlooked five billowing mill smokestacks from my office window.

The people of the town were sturdy and hearty, closely confined in their mentality, but highly intelligent in their capacity to make the things around them work. They relished conversation over fixing this or that at the plant or creating some gadget they wanted at home. They were practical-minded people.

Conversation about world events or current ideas was somewhere between hopeless and impossible.

The U.S. Army conscripted Covington youth in great numbers. Especially when there was national conflict, hundreds of "our boys" would trek off to see the world from a troop carrier. Military deaths dotted every generation. The community had a special ritual, and the cemetery had special markers, for local sons who had died in the defense of our freedom.

Life's greatest aspirations were tied to sports. Just enough local kids made it big—perhaps one every fifteen years—to provide the youngsters with dreams and the oldsters with lore. The whole town would tune in the baseball Game of the Week on summer Saturday afternoons, especially if a native son was on the mound. An unparalleled moment in the community's life happened on the rare occasions when one of these locally bred successes would come back home to visit—a pitcher with the Indians, or a linebacker with the Giants! The radio station, the weekly newspaper, the entire community would

4

ring with celebration. You enjoyed the greatest personal status in those moments if one of these returning super-stars actually knew your name, because you had been "part o' his raisin'." The experience would provide an emotional lift for several years.

I enjoyed devoted, happy relationships in Covington. The people were kind, good-hearted, and fundamentally honest, and they would do anything to support their pas-tor. But these years were virtually devoid of challenges to the mind. There was no inquiry into larger worlds, no uncovering of thoughts and ideas we had never thought before.

A seventeen-year-old girl told me one summer that she was spending her vacation working on several books. "What are you reading?" I asked hopefully.

"I'm not reading anything," she replied. "I'm trying to finish three coloring books I bought in Roanoke."

The clearest picture of life in this place appeared before my eyes at 10:45 one weeknight. I had been down to the YMCA coffee shop for a late snack, and I was motoring my 1960 Volkswagen back through town toward my apart-ment. As I turned a corner, my headlights illumined three male figures walking toward me on the opposite side of the street. All three had on work clothes and carried lunch boxes, headed for the graveyard shift at the paper mill. All three were members of my congregation, men I knew: grandfather, father, and son. It occurred to me: three generations with no larger imagination than to spend their lives in this circumscribed little mountain pit. "Doesn't anyone ever get out of here?"

And yet, embodied in this threesome was a community the world beyond had sacrificed. These men knew one another, intertwined with one another, cared about one another, loved and hated one another — intimately, constantly, personally. When a reward was won, they all celebrated; when a loss was suffered, no one suffered alone. Here, in vivid color before my eyes, was a vital human network called family, something the chic, upscale world of the new America would soon be paying millions of dollars in therapists' fees in a vain effort to re-create. Here was relationship, the ultimate purpose of human life. I was touched.

I began this work at age twenty-four, a seminary student, new and green. I had never known of a husband who beat his wife, never watched the ravaging effect of alcoholism on family relationships. I had no idea what an aneurysm was. I did not know about midlife crises or postpartum depression. I was idealistic, eager, trying to be a pastor to people thirty or more years older than I. I had very little confidence in what I was doing. I remember feeling like an intruder, even though there was nothing in the community's welcome that should have made me feel that way.

I include in this section four stories from life in Covington. Three came from the personal lives of church members. The fourth, "Skeered of One Another," tells of an event in the community's life.

A Garland Instead of Ashes

Rain pelted hard against the window of the Greyhound bus, casting sprays of water that turned everything outside into formless shadows. Occasional lights passed — a porch light from a farmhouse, a street lamp, the headlights of an oncoming car — but it was impossible for Loretta to make out anything clearly. The blurred darkness reflected the feeling within her. Yes, everything had been very successful so far. Her departure was proceeding smoothly. But in this moment, a moment of calm on the bus, she became acutely aware of being lost. She did not know where she was, and she did not have the slightest idea where she was going. She was frightened, terrified, in a way she could not afford to admit. Seven-year-old Sonny and four-year-old Mary Pat slept on the seat beside her. She had to stay strong. They depended on her. She had to carry them all through. She could not be taken over by her fear.

Loretta had grown up in a West Virginia holler. With a fifth-grade education, she had ventured into the outside world only a few times, and then only as far as the town on the main road. She had been fifteen when she married Billy Ray, who was eighteen. Billy Ray had had a silly streak that made her laugh. For example, there was the day he brought home a blacksnake that had caught itself in a wire fence. He suggested that they nurse it back to health in their bathtub; he insisted on giving Loretta snake-handling lessons.

But Billy Ray also had a temper, set off especially by alcohol. Loretta learned to beware when Billy Ray came home in the evenings from his truck driving job, because he usually stopped for what he called a "quick beer." Most evenings it was all right, but now and then it wasn't. Loretta had learned to read the signs, to know when to slip away to spend the night with her close friend, Brenda, who lived nearby.

After Sonny and then Mary Pat had been born, however, Loretta couldn't slip away so easily. When Billy Ray came home drunk, she would have to bear his abuse: arguing, shouting, accusing her, and then, in due time, slapping and punching her. He was always sorry the next morning — couldn't believe what he had done to his own wife! — but it never stopped him from drinking the next night.

The first time Billy Ray lit into five-year-old Sonny, Loretta realized she had to do something. Sonny had been asleep when his father had come home, and for some unexplained reason his father had wanted him awake. Billy Ray had yanked the boy up, shaken him, shouted at him and thrown him back on the bed — with Loretta clawing at Billy Ray's arms. Sonny had been so terrorized that for weeks afterward he had fought desperately against going to sleep. Every instinct in Loretta's mind and heart was focused on taking care of these children. The next day Loretta had started hiding away dollar bills in an old Morton Salt container for the day when she would need them.

The time had come earlier than she anticipated. Billy Ray had come home one night in a rage — he and one of his friends had had an argument. He had nearly broken the front door off its hinges coming in. He had attacked her in a corner of the kitchen, leaving her bruised and bloody. He had smashed several objects in the front room, including two old lamps and his daughter's doll. He had then stormed through the children's bedroom, leaving them cowering in fear beneath his verbal assault. After he had finally sunk into his chair, Loretta had eased over to a neighbor's house to recruit help in keeping him calm. She had also vowed that this would be the last night she and the children would spend with Billy Ray. She would let him go off to his three o'clock to eleven o'clock shift the next afternoon, and as quickly as possible she and the children would be gone. She did not know where to go, but there had to be a place better than this.

Brenda had taken them to the bus depot—Loretta could trust Brenda. Brenda had heard that there was a town beyond the Virginia line, and even though she didn't know anything about it, she thought Loretta might find a new start there. Lacking any other plan, Loretta had decided to try it. Thus was she on this Greyhound bus, frightened and lost, having no idea what would happen but determined that whatever it was had to work. She had crossed through the waters of the Red Sea, and she was not going back to the slavery of Egypt.

At one point the bus was stopped by people outside. The driver opened the door and talked to someone. "Are they searching for me already?" she thought tensely. "Billy Ray shouldn't even be home from work yet." No, it was something else. The rain had caused a crack in the road, and vehicles were being steered around it. She felt better once they reached the other side, thinking that the road problem would slow Billy Ray down, too.

Leading her two weary children down the steps of the bus at 9:15 P.M., she stood on a rain-soaked sidewalk deciding what to do next. There were no welcome mats in her promised land, only the darkened streets of a paper-mill town already shut down for the night. A bleak beginning. She managed to read partially burned-out neon letters in a window two blocks away: "H-O-T-E-L." "Maybe that's where to start," she thought to herself.

It was a modest place, an old YMCA, but it looked good to Loretta. Leading her children in the door, she had to call out several times to attract the owner's attention. He was not expecting anyone. "I don't have much money," she said, "but I will work for you if you will give me and my children a place to stay." The owner regarded them, seeing the bruises on her face and piecing together what

9

was going on. He knew what could happen in these mountains, and this one was pretty easy to read. "Room 12," he said, "down the hall on your left; and you can work in the restaurant tomorrow. We've been needing someone."

Loretta lay in bed with her children that night, singing quiet songs, bone weary from the journey but thankful that they were safe and dry. She fed them from the bag of food she had brought. After the children drifted off to sleep, she slid to her knees by the bed and prayed with all her strength that God would take care of them. She gazed at the ceiling, following the cracks that meandered through the plaster and wondering where they led. She read her Bible, searching for words of guidance.

The next day she embarked on her new career: as cook, waitress, checkout clerk, and anything else needed in the restaurant. It wasn't much, but Loretta was the kind of person who could make herself happy on not much.

Several months later — with Sonny enrolled in school and Mary Pat making a life out of mimicking her mother — a man came into the restaurant one night and ordered dinner. He smiled at Loretta and cast a fond glance at Mary Pat. The next night he was back. And a third night. This time he introduced himself as Howard. By the fifth night they had fallen into friendly conversation.

Howard was a construction supervisor specializing in school buildings. He moved here and there across western Virginia, wherever his boss needed him. He had been married once, but things had not worked out. Now he was just a single guy, working to keep the wolf from the door. He seemed pleasant, easy to get along with. But Loretta knew about men: they could be one thing one moment and something entirely different the next. She cautioned herself to proceed with great care.

Howard did not seem in a rush. He had within him a bedrock belief that whatever was right would finally come about, and he seemed happy to wait.

They enjoyed each other. Howard would take Loretta and the children for rides: to the state park, to the lake, even to Roanoke, where they were totally awed by the magnitude of everything. Loretta would fix Howard special meals at the restaurant; meat loaf with mashed potatoes and gravy was his favorite. Howard began taking Loretta to his church, where she met new friends and liked it a lot.

Six months became a year. Howard was as devoted a companion as one could wish for, but he still did not press her. Finally, one night, he said to Loretta, "I love you, Loretta; will you marry me?" Her heart stopped, overcome with joy but also seized by the greatest foreboding. "Where will this lead?" she wondered. She returned to the hotel room that night and prayed the most fervent prayer of her life. "Lord, show me the way! Help me do the best for my children! Help me do the best for me and Howard! Will things change if we get married? I don't want to get swept off my feet and land in the mud again! Tell me what to do!"

God spoke to Loretta that night, and the message was anything but nondirective. "Loretta, it was courage, not fear, that brought you out of that holler. You asked me for the strength to overcome your fears, and I gave it to you. Don't fail me now! Don't come this far and then turn back." The next night, Loretta said yes to Howard.

She thought about whether she was about to end up married to two men. She thought there was some law against that. But the fact was that Billy Ray had never actually gotten around to buying a marriage license—at least if he had, she had never signed it—so she didn't think she had anything to worry about. And, besides that, how well did Pocahontas County, West Virginia, keep up with holler marriages in 1951?

Howard and Loretta had a joyous wedding! The kids loved Howard, and the church loved Loretta. They moved into Howard's four-room garage apartment, a lot more spacious than the hotel room. With Mary Pat now in school, Loretta continued to work at the restaurant, partly because they could use the extra income, and partly because she still felt very grateful to the man who had helped her that first night.

Despite the joy, however, Loretta kept a bit of reserve. She remembered how things had changed with Billy Ray. She would still wake up in the night dreaming about those horrible moments, and she wondered if the same thing could happen again. She didn't share much of her fear with Howard; she didn't want her past stamping an ugly blotch on their happiness. But the idea hung around.

Then one Saturday a letter arrived from Brenda. Billy Ray had started asking a lot of questions, Brenda said. At first he had tried to act like Loretta's leaving didn't matter to him, trying to show that he was big and tough and could take anything. But now, two years later, he wanted to know where his wife and kids were. At the bus depot, at the post office, among Loretta's friends, Billy Ray had been asking questions. Brenda thought Loretta should keep an eye out in case he found out something. This news upset Loretta. It made every knock at the door and every venture outside the house a wary experience. She wished she could learn more from Brenda, but it was too dangerous.

Early one Monday morning, Howard left for a five-day trek to his current work site, eighty-five miles away—too far to commute each night. He had stayed away before, but never had it made Loretta feel so lonely and threatened. All week she wondered what might happen. On Thursday another letter arrived in the mail, but it was not from Brenda but from Howard. He had never written before, and Loretta wondered why he was writing now. He would be home in two days. As she walked up the apartment steps from the mailbox, her fears crowded in around her. She managed to get herself inside the door and to sit down before she opened the letter.

It read: "Dear Loretta. Everything is fine here, and the job is going well. I noticed before I left that you got a letter from Brenda, and that it seemed to upset you. I don't know what she said — maybe I don't want to know — but whatever it was, I want you to know that I love you. Together we will make it; don't worry about anything else. I'll be home Saturday. All my love — Howard." From that moment, Loretta knew that there was no longer any need for fear.

The prophet Isaiah, in the sixth century B.C.E., spoke redemption to a people beaten and broken, a nation that had been exiled for forty years in a foreign land:

> The Spirit of the Lord is upon me;
>> the Lord has anointed me.
> to bring good news to the oppressed,
>> to bind up the brokenhearted;
> to proclaim liberty to the captives,
>> release to the prisoners;
> to proclaim the year of the Lord's favor,
>> to comfort all who mourn.
> To provide good things for those who weep,
>> a garland instead of ashes,
> the oil of gladness rather than tears of mourning,
>> a mantle of rejoicing instead of a faint spirit.
> They shall be called oaks of righteousness,
>> the planting of the Lord, to display God's glory.
>
> Isaiah 61:1–3

Twenty-seven hundred years later, the promise is still kept!

For six weeks one year it was my privilege and pleasure to live with Loretta and Howard in the downstairs room of their garage apartment. They were also honored guests when my wife and I were married.

Skeered of One Another

The news swept the town. Two young men, strangers dressed in jeans and T-shirts, had arrived the night before on the Greyhound bus. With duffel bags in hand, they had hailed a cab. Directing the cabbie to head west on the main road, they had disappeared.

Later that evening the sheriff spotted a cab parked by the side of the road about three miles out of town. Thinking it strange, he stopped to look. On the ground on the far side of the cab he found the driver, dead from gunshots to the chest, robbed of what little money he had been carrying. It was a horrifying scene: a brutal murder for the sake of a few bucks. These kids must have borne no regard for human life. A couple of drifters who killed a respected community resident, a husband and father of three, for nothing more than their next meal. What else would they do and to whom? Obviously, nothing was beyond them.

And where were they now? The cab was parked by the road. There had been no reports of stolen vehicles. No further sightings. They had to be still close by. Were they on foot? Had they taken to the mountains, the vast areas of untouched hillside that dominated the region? Were they wandering somewhere up above in search of their next victim? The sheriff suspected they had been around on the other side of the cab while he was tending to the dead man—he had heard suspicious noises at one point. It was all eerie and shocking for a small town where everyone knew one another and things like this did not happen. The community was electrified! It became the first thing on everyone's lips. No baseball scores, no paper-mill talk, no wondering how soon the next rain would come to wash down the town. Just, "the murder," the horrid reality of what seemed unreal. It filled the breakfast coffee joints, the barbershops, the YMCA, the bars, the street-corner conversations, the local radio.

Rumors abounded. The two had appeared in a little grocery store on the edge of town, bought some food, and left before anyone could call the police. They had circled back into town and had been spotted stalking the swimming pool, probably hoping to abduct a teenage girl to rape and murder her. They had come by a church asking for money but had disappeared quickly when the janitor had said he would have to call someone else. They had been in the woods outside the drive-in restaurant, obviously hoping to steal a car by killing its occupants. They had stolen several guns from a farmhouse where the family was away, and they were preparing to make a nighttime assault on people's homes.

Tension abounded in the community. One family I visited had rifles and shotguns spread all around the dining room, cleaning them. A woman showed me the revolver she kept in the drawer by her bed, and a second woman showed me the pistol she kept in her kitchen utility cabinet. Neighbors did not sit on the front porch quite as much or amble the sidewalks at night with the same abandon. Car doors were kept locked, house doors bolted. Bars went up over windows. Anyone caring for small children kept special vigil. Strange noises were carefully noted and investigated.

One night one of my church members bolted out of bed and grabbed his shotgun. He had been awakened by footsteps outside his bedroom window. Gazing vigilantly through the curtain with gun poised, he had seen the backs of two men. It took him a moment before he realized that he recognized them. They were his neighbors, walking up the sidewalk, heading home from the second shift at the paper mill, just as they had done for the past twenty-three years. On most nights their proximity would have caused him to feel more secure; on this night he had felt terror.

One man outside town fired shots at a movement he could not identify in the grove of trees across the street from his house.

I shared a small house with another unmarried pastor. We lived seven miles out of town, in a tiny village clustered around what used to be a local foundry. Someone in our village obtained a topographic map of the area, plotted the mountain ridges, and announced that one ridge led exactly from where the murder had occurred around to our community. Someone had thought they spotted a couple of strange men in the woods above us and figured that the murderers had followed that ridge. The village froze! Were the murderers overhead? Would they sneak down some night and brutally slaughter us?

I remember most vividly the night of the barking dog. My housemate owned a giant, very rambunctious boxer named Caesar. Caesar spent most of his time chained to a long clothesline in our backyard, which didn't help his temperament. I, and the whole village, hated Caesar because whenever he ran loose — usually once each evening — he jumped fences without even breaking stride, terrorized children, and drooled all over everyone. I used to despise it when my housemate would let Caesar inside at night; I had either to cloister myself in my bedroom or spend the next two hours fending off a slobbering dog.

One night shortly after the murder, when my housemate was out of town, Caesar started barking in the backyard at 2:00 A.M. He rarely did that. I awakened wondering what or whom he had heard. We lived at the end of a village road with the mountain ridge straight above our backyard, and we had never before now locked the doors. Caesar kept barking. It was chilling. I had discounted the community rumor, but at 2:00 A.M. things seem a lot less certain than in the daylight. That was the one night— the only night—I personally decided to let Caesar inside, thinking it would be better to have him roaming the house with me than chained safely out of reach in the backyard.

One afternoon during that time I was driving out the road west of town with a teenage boy named Gary from my church. We passed a covey of about five Virginia State Police cars at the spot where the murder had occurred. Gary commented, "The murder scene."

"Awful," I replied.

My 1960 Volkswagen had no gas gauge; everything in that finely built little car was designed for minimum cost. What it did have was a crank beneath the dashboard. If you ran out of gas, you turned that crank a quarter turn, and you suddenly had an extra gallon. It worked fine as long as you had remembered to return the crank to its regular position when you filled up. This was one of two times in the thirteen years I owned that car that I forgot to turn the crank back. About a quarter mile beyond the murder scene, just around a bend, I felt the Volkswagen run out of gas. I reached down to turn the crank, and it was already turned—we were truly out of gas. Gary and I puttered to the side of the road.

We were both aware of feeling a bit uneasy at being stuck here, of all places! As we walked along the roadside back toward the Virginia troopers, we saw them first spot us. They didn't exactly circle the wagons, but they also did not cordially welcome us. We wondered for a moment from which direction came the greatest danger.

Gary explained that he lived in town, and I said that I was a pastor in the local Presbyterian church. My North Carolina driver's license didn't help any—they had an innate suspicion of anyone from beyond the border— but, after several suspicious once-overs, one trooper said, "C'mon, I'll run you to the gas station." From there we had a good conversation.

I stand in the greatest awe of people who possess the magical talent of being able to read the moment, people who, when they find themselves in the middle of a situation, can size up accurately what is going on. There are a few people in this world who are a lot better at it than most of the rest of us. It is not a capacity bestowed by education; some of the most degreed people I know are essentially dumb at knowing what is going on around them. It is not a talent developed by intention. I cannot decide I want to be able to do it and develop the knack. A few people simply have it. Those few who do, I find fascinating.

There was a gentleman called Ole Fred who lived in town. Devoid of polish, Ole Fred nevertheless had a quick wit and a sharp humor. He always knew the latest stories and never tired of sharing them. At seventy-five or so, he just hung around public places and talked to people. He would wander into the drugstore, the YMCA, the town restaurant, and pick up with whoever was there. He even came to church on occasion, not talking a whole lot because he believed religion to be too complicated and controversial for him to talk about.

Over coffee about two mornings after the murder, Ole Fred commented to the mayor, "We've done got so skeered o' one another 'round here that someone's gonna hurt someone." That was the greatest favor Ole Fred ever did for Covington. Perceptive words! Accurate prophecy! Everyone else had the fever—jump out of your skin at every noise—but Ole Fred had sat back and surveyed the full situation, and he was more skeered of us than of "them."

His words flipped a switch in the mayor's head—something that didn't happen too often. The mayor stewed around for a couple of hours and then decided what to do.

The town had a loud, emergency siren that went off whenever someone phoned for the fire truck or the ambulance. As soon as that siren wailed, people all over town would switch on their radios, because the radio station would report where the crisis was and what was going on.

About 11:00 A.M. on this day, the siren wailed. Even more people than usual turned on their radios, because everyone wondered if the murderers had done something else or been caught. What they heard on this occasion was neither. They heard the mayor, making a speech to the city—the only time anyone could recall the siren being used this way.

Our mayor was a genial old mountain gentleman, well regarded by many but not known for leading anyone anywhere they had not been before. "Keeping things stable"

19

was his motto. It never occurred to him to think new thoughts or imagine his community anywhere other than where it was.

But when the radios went on, here came the mayor exclaiming, "We've done got so skeered o' one another 'round here that someone's gonna hurt someone." He followed this statement with an impassioned pronouncement that the police were doing everything they could to track the murderers, that the community needed to trust the police to take care of things, that 99 percent of the stories making their way around were untrue, that we should put our guns away and stop jumping at every noise, that these two young men had "skeered" our community so much that we had become a menace to ourselves. It was one of the most noble, heroic speeches I have ever heard from a politician. He was not trying to win votes in the next election; he was simply trying to prevent us from killing one another. Hardly could it be classified as an eloquent speech — it was, in fact, jerky and halting — but there was no mistaking the intensity behind it. This man was concerned for his town, and he was pleading with us to start acting differently before his concerns became real.

The town got the message. Soon Ole Fred's words were everywhere. At the hardware store: "We've done got so skeered o' one another 'round here that someone's gonna hurt someone." At the beauty parlor: "We've done got so skeered o' one another 'round here that someone's gonna hurt someone." Even the Sunday morning preachers took it up: "We've done got so skeered o' one another 'round here that someone's gonna hurt someone."

How, why, does a piece of insight catch on and sweep a community, transforming it into something new?

The community returned to its front porches that night, breathed fresh air, and put away its guns. It also perceived something important: that the most dangerous beast of all is the beast that lives within, that our own quest for security is often more dangerous than the threat from which we seek to be secured.

Three days after it all began, the sheriff's deputies captured their suspects. Straight up the hill three hundred yards from where the murder had occurred: two bedraggled nineteen-year-old boys sitting against a rock overlooking the feverish activity in the road below. Gary and I, as we had walked up the road, had passed directly beneath their view. With food scraps here and there and nearly no water, they just sat. The murder weapon lay on the rock. They hadn't gone anywhere. The capture was too easy for all the work and emotion that had gone into it.

But the community breathed a great collective sigh of relief that night, glad that this encounter with itself was finally over.

Amy's Gift

Amy, age ten, lived with her sister and brother-in-law. A young fawn in the spring of life, it was nothing short of hideous when she was diagnosed with acute leukemia. A ten-year-old is supposed to ride bicycles, read books, play with dogs, swim, do acrobatics, concoct imaginary plots, and giggle with her friends, not lie in a hospital bed with her hair falling out.

Amy lived with her sister, Carol, because their mother, Rhonda, was what the local community called "a honky-tonk woman," a gypsy with incurable wanderlust. In her late teens, Rhonda had been married long enough to bear Carol. Then she had disappeared, leaving Carol's father to raise their daughter. Word would come from Rhonda every now and then: she was in Vegas, she was in Reno, she was in L.A. — getting along but not too well; always conveying a touch of pathos, always thinking of coming home. But she never did, until Carol was twenty years old. Then, suddenly, for no known reason, Rhonda showed up, filled with remorse, begging forgiveness, wanting to start over with her husband and daughter and to work out a happy life.

Father, the one ever to forgive, had received her back, not knowing what to make of this unexpected enlivening of his life but willing to try. Carol had been more skeptical; she had resented her mother's absence throughout her childhood, and setting aside her anger was not going to happen quickly. Besides that, she found Rhonda cheap, tacky, and transparent, not at all a person Carol could be proud of. In her deepest heart, Carol wished her mother would go away again.

After eleven months at home, and at age thirty-nine, Rhonda bore Amy. Within four months, Rhonda was gone again. It was the same story. Rhonda couldn't be harnessed to one place very long. She needed the bright lights, the nightlife, the adventure.

She again communicated now and then, but less often. She sent the same messages: getting along but not too well; thinking of coming home. Father and Carol had learned to disregard it all.

Carol had taken Amy; Dad really didn't have a clue. Carol also had married Jake, a strong, dependable guy, and they had begun to create their own family. Amy became their oldest child.

All had gone well until Amy was diagnosed with leukemia. The news had wrenched everyone. It was terrible. From that point forward, the family had reoriented its entire life toward taking care of this frequently ill child who was going to die. They managed as gracefully as one could hope.

Amy tried to live normally but was often in the hospital. She didn't entirely know what was happening to her, and she developed a kind of placid distance that enabled her to ignore the parts of her life she didn't want to understand. I visited her at home and in the hospital; she tended to be cordial in her childlike way but not warm. I repeatedly had the feeling that she wanted me to keep a distance from her emotions, a request I honored.

It was different with Carol. Carol reached out for all the support she could get. She had to struggle constantly with the demands of daily existence, and she was of no mind to do it alone. She would tell the stories of what had happened, her feelings, her fears. I came to feel that I knew Carol well. She was the type of person who would tearfully describe everything and then go back to her duties with renewed vigor. None of the hard questions ever got answered, but telling the story seemed to do a lot for her.

One evening my phone rang. It was Carol, obvious irritation in her voice: "We're at the hospital. It looks like we're close to the end. Things are pretty bad here. Can you come?" I went.

I arrived to find Carol out in the hallway seething with anger. She explained, "My mother showed up this afternoon! No one knows how or why. She said she just had a feeling something was wrong, that she was needed here. She hasn't communicated in two years, so she didn't know anything about Amy. She came to the house first, and a neighbor told her we were at the hospital.

"As soon as she walked in and saw Amy, she went to pieces. Amy is in a coma, and I hope to God she doesn't know what's going on around her. I'm afraid she does. Mother is all over the room, crying, pouting, running her mouth incessantly. I stayed in there for a while, but then I couldn't stand it any longer. I tried to bring her out with me, but she only replied, 'This is my child! My baby!' If she is so concerned with 'her baby,' why wasn't she around during the past ten years to help raise her? I am so angry I can't face her any longer. I came outside just to keep from blowing up. Go in and see for yourself; you won't believe it. And when you come out, try to bring her with you!"

I slipped into the hospital room. Amy lay motionless, her eyes slightly open but glazed. Her graying cast confirmed that we were indeed probably near the end. Rhonda was boundless nervousness, everywhere at once, exclaiming, lamenting. "O my dear baby, I have neglected you! I have spent my life away. I should have been here. I should have been here with you. God led me here so I could at least see you alive. O my dear baby, forgive me! God forgives me; can you forgive me? God said to this poor wretched woman, 'Come home!' I have come home, and it is not too late. Great Lord in heaven, bring me close to my daughter. Help her to take me back into her heart. O my dear precious baby. You are the light of my life, the love of my heart. I need you. I need your love, your touch, your forgiveness. Forgive me Lord, forgive me precious one. I need your forgiveness so much. I have been awful, terrible. I have drifted. I have taken up here and there. I have been away while my child was growing, when my child became sick. Forgive me, God; forgive me, baby. Take me back into your heart before it is too late."

A few times in my life I have seen litanies that apparently had no end. This was one. After perhaps fifteen minutes, I broke in and addressed Rhonda aggressively, "I am James Chatham, a pastor to the family."

"A pastor!" Mother replied. "A pastor. You are wonderful to come. We need you so much. What a fine person you are. I know you have your own family, your own children going to bed about now. But you are here, helping us. How can we ever thank you enough? It's wonderful of you!" I think it was in that moment that I first realized that I needed to disregard the effusive praise of guilt-ridden people who want to project me as a model of everything they aren't. It would happen to me at other times as well. It is one of the hazards of being a pastor.

I guided Rhonda to a chair and got her seated. She continued to jerk and mumble and make strange noises, but at least she was calming down. I sat beside her for several minutes, both of us watching Amy. Still no motion, simply glazed eyes. Finally Rhonda seemed to relax. The feverishness went out of her, and she settled more calmly into her chair. I didn't know how long she would stay that way.

Carol, sensing the quiet, slipped back inside the room. Glancing at me, she mouthed, "What did you do?" I smiled to convey that we were doing all right, at least for now.

We all sat there together quietly: Mother closest to Amy, with Carol and me on either side, no one saying anything.

Then, one of the most remarkable events I have ever experienced anytime, anywhere took place. How it happened I do not know; it was beyond anyone's understanding. I still stand in awe of this moment. Amy moved slightly, shifting her head. Her eyes seemed to gather themselves and focus. She looked, puzzled at first and then more clearly, with knowing recognition. She almost twinkled, happy, surprised. She spoke, "Mother, I'm glad you are here." She pulled her mother's hand to her face for a brief moment.

How could Amy know who Rhonda was? Amy had not seen her mother since she was four months old. It was impossible. But she knew.

That's all she said: "Mother, I'm glad you are here." Then she drifted back out again.

Healing words! Miraculous words! An entire team of psychotherapists could not have devised anything better.

Amy did not seem to have taken in the wailing and lamentation that had gone on over the past two hours. If she had said, "Mother, I forgive you," we would have known she had heard, and it would have been exceedingly bad. It also would have meant nothing — too easy, phony.

But her words were sincere, authentic, heartfelt: "Mother, I'm glad you are here."

That small utterance changed everything! No longer obsessed with the weeping and wailing, Carol, in one of the more heroic acts I have ever seen, actually eased over to her mother and said, "I'm glad you are here, too." Rhonda seemed to experience the forgiveness she needed; her heart calmed.

After a bit, we all walked outside the room and down the hall, clinging to one another as if we had all just witnessed a miracle. I think we had.

It would be an uneasy truce between Carol and Rhonda, but things were different now. Carol would tell this story proudly, the first pride she had ever taken in her mother.

This happened around 9:40 P.M. At 2:15 A.M., Amy died, quietly, with no further communication. In her death, she had left her gift, a gift of healing: "Mother, I'm glad you are here." I wonder to this day where that moment came from.

Rhonda stayed for the funeral but then left again, saying she had unfinished business in California. It was probably good. The best thing that could happen already had.

I do not focus my life on miracles. I find that doing so quickly becomes both annoying and self-centered. I don't really want an explanation for what happened that night, and I do not wish to command the power to make it happen again. "Miracles" have been an enormous retail business across the South, making their most glitzy practitioners wealthy beyond measure. I was amused several years ago when a friend in my home state of North Carolina told me that the three largest income-producing industries in the state were tobacco, textiles, and miracle religion. I am not interested.

I have, however, witnessed in my life two or three miracle moments, Amy's gift being one. I prefer to stand my distance from those moments, not wishing to examine them too closely, not wanting to invade their sacredness, letting them maintain their status as holy ground. I am deeply thankful for them. They add a rich dimension to my life. They let me know that what I discern and understand on this planet is but a tiny, tiny piece of the whole reality. That is enough.

Springtime in the Mountains

Rita's only child, Dewayne, was killed in Vietnam. He had been a meek, mild-natured boy, the kind who could be present in a room for several hours before you realized he was there. When he went off to the military, everyone wondered if this little kid would simply get lost in the numbers, never to reemerge. But that's not what happened at all. Meek, mild little Dewayne threw himself on a grenade in a Vietnam ditch trying to save his buddies. He received, posthumously, a congressional medal for his heroism.

Four months later, Rita's husband, Jacob, was scorched over 90 percent of his body when he jumped on a boiler top that was threatening to tip off at the paper mill. He, like his son, was trying to protect his fellow workers. The accident could have spewed steaming liquid all across the factory floor. Jacob survived three weeks in great agony before an infection finally claimed him. The parade of appreciative, supportive, empathetic coworkers never ceased during that time.

Rita was shattered! She was suddenly alone at age thirty-nine, no son, no husband. She missed them dreadfully; they had been her life. The shock had numbed her for a while, but then she fell into deep depression. She lived in her bathrobe, barely able to get out of bed and make her way through the day. Every idea she had about getting some activity started seemed so overwhelming that she dismissed it. She checked out some books from the library but was unable to get herself to read. Her friends would drop by and attempt conversation, but they found her little more than a shriveled shell of the woman she had been. She dropped from 132 pounds to 103. She stopped coming to Sunday school and church despite repeated attempts by church members to reach out to her. Her car would sit in her driveway for days, unmoved. There was no psychiatrist or therapist within fifty miles, and even if there had been, this community would have considered a shrink a frivolous waste of hard-earned money.

Nothing improved with Rita. She had been a reserved woman all her life, and now she became more so, withdrawing further each day into her isolated shell.

One day her friend Hazel decided that things had gone on long enough. Hazel had never been timid. Now the time had come for her best performance. She marched in one morning, sat on Rita's living room sofa and announced — it was not a question but an announcement — "Rita, you and I are going to grow flowers together, starting now. You raise the prettiest flowers in the state of Virginia. Everyone wonders how you and those gorgeous little blossoms get along so well. As soon as they see your face, they come popping out like they're trying to please you. I don't care how you're feeling, honey. I don't care what kind of mood you're in. I don't care what you think of what I'm saying to you. It's springtime in the mountains. You're gonna march yourself into that bedroom, get rid of that dingy old bathrobe you wear all the time, put on your jeans and work shirt, and you and I are going out in your backyard to plant flowers." Hazel labeled it "dirt therapy," declaring that it was God's original gift to Adam and Eve, the most effective medicine ever devised for the human spirit.

Hazel was relentless, not sympathetic to any of Rita's protests. In the mornings, Hazel would push her way in, declaring that regardless of how either of them felt, those flowers craved friendship. One morning when Rita declared that she just didn't feel like doing anything that day, Hazel created a song, "Just Don't Feel Like Doing Nothing Today," and bounced all over the house singing it playfully. She then grabbed up Rita and began the "Just Don't Feel Like Doing Nothing Today Boogie," which finally convinced the dazed Rita that she had no choice.

On other days, Hazel would arrange for two or three of Rita's friends to drop by in work clothes to spend a couple of hours pulling weeds, feeding plants, watering, and talking about what was happening in town.

Hazel and Rita turned Rita's yard into a showcase of color: daisies, zinnias, vinca, sweet william, impatiens, begonias, geraniums; red, yellow, white, blue, lavender, orange, and purple — the works. Cars would stop out front to gaze over the back fence to glimpse the beauty. The garden club in the neighborhood where the paper mill's management lived even sent representatives to see what everyone was talking about over on the labor hill.

And not only did those flowers come to life; Rita came to life too. The dreariness of her depression began to be sparked by rays of light. One of the friends told a story of preparing for her teenage daughter's first date, and Rita found herself actually laughing. She began to look forward to working in the garden and seeing her friends. She discovered that she could still live for other people, love other people. Her loss never went away — she struggled with her memories — but good things also began to show up.

Hazel had figured out exactly the right medicine. No one else could have made it happen that way. A little well-calculated audacity sometimes works wonders.

Not only did Rita's flowers come to life, but so did Rita. Springtime in the mountains came for both of them.

Fayette and Union
Church, Mississippi
1964–1966

On Sunday, June 28, 1964, my wife, Nancy, and I drove along Interstate 20 from Alabama into Mississippi. Three days later, I was officially to take up duties as pastor of the Fayette and Union Church Presbyterian churches in the southwest part of the state. We were traveling in our 1960 black Volkswagen beetle, and we were hot.

We had been married on June 21, seven days earlier. Also on June 21, three civil rights workers, Michael Schwerner, Andrew Goodman, and James Chaney, had been murdered on a rural road in Neshoba County, Mississippi. The three were part of Freedom Summer, a 1964 project of the Council of Federated Organizations (COFO), which included several civil rights groups. Freedom Summer was bringing into Mississippi nearly a thousand volunteer young people to set up freedom schools and conduct voter-registration drives. The burned-out shell of the station wagon driven by the three young men had been found two days after the murders. It would be several weeks before their bodies would be discovered buried in an earthen dam. Several local Ku Klux Klansmen, including a deputy sheriff, would later be charged with the murders.

The first thing Nancy and I encountered as we crossed into our newly adopted state was an enormous military convoy, perhaps four hundred trucks, jeeps, personnel carriers, and other vehicles bringing equipment and men into Mississippi. We drove for several miles trying to get around this slow-moving line. We had the distinct feeling that we were entering a war zone, that the state was under siege.

Until this moment, the Neshoba County violence had felt far enough away. We had read about it in the newspapers and seen it on television. But despite the fact that we would soon be moving into Mississippi, the horror had always seemed somewhere else. Until now. Staring into the face of that military convoy, we knew. There were people near us willing to kill (Neshoba County was thirty-eight miles up the road). Those people were very angry and very upset, vindictive toward anyone from the outside. We were clearly outsiders, two young people in a Volkswagen bearing a North Carolina license plate. Did we have any idea what we were doing?

That was our first impression of Mississippi. Our second impression came soon afterward. We drove halfway across the state on the interstate highway and then turned southward on a lesser road. The scenery was unforgettable. For long stretches, distances that seemed interminable, we saw nothing but desolation, miles and miles of bleakness: small wooden shacks, deteriorated barns, dirt yards, dirt side roads, no electricity, kerosene lanterns, rusted shells of cars, beaten-up mailboxes, at best a few flowers in the corner of a yard, and dust everywhere — an almost total barrenness. We had known that Mississippi was the economically poorest state in the nation, but we had not known the reality of what that would mean. We felt like we were entering a time machine and stepping back a century.

And then there was the kudzu, the massive, ubiquitous, aggressive fields of kudzu, acting as if it were on the verge of taking over the state. In some places, it climbed over everything: banks, buildings, trees, telephone poles, roadways. It seemed to have a relentless appetite, and it was always in search of additional growing space.

Fayette was a town of sixteen hundred in southwest Mississippi. Its leadership consisted mostly of farm owners, people who ran small agricultural businesses on the rather sizable land plots they had inherited from their ancestors. The town consisted of one stoplight, a carefully tended Confederate memorial park, three gas stations that took turns staying open on weekends, two restaurants, two grocery stores, a hardware store, a drugstore, a laundry, a funeral home, and fourteen churches. The county's population was 80 percent black.

I came to like Fayette's easy transportation — there was barely a need for a car — and the small-town familiarity. I liked the shade roofs that extended over the sidewalks from the midtown buildings. I liked the massive live oak trees that created interesting silhouettes on the horizon. I liked the baseball games that were played at night on the Little League field across from our backyard. And I liked the pace of life; only rarely was anyone in a hurry.

But there was much more going on in Fayette. We were eighteen miles from Natchez, the historic capital of the Deep South's social aura. The glory era of southern aristocracy had long since passed, the time when fine families of grace and wealth dominated the region. Plantation culture was dead. And yet Fayette, as a pale reflection of Natchez, continued to live the pretense that the past had never changed. It clung to the myth of a hundred years earlier that "our way of life" bore a natural superiority over all others. Rich, southern graciousness, we pretended, was still the ideal way.

It was possible to believe this myth only because of the region's acute isolation. The area carried on very little interchange with the wider world. Fayette was proud of its isolation, disparaging the degraded lifestyles and moral decay of the outside world and wanting no part in it. We saw ourselves as an island of southern superiority that others should wish to copy.

The aristocratic families sensed deep down, however, that they were living a sham, that their world had failed and would not regain its ascendancy. It was perfectly obvious that the glory of the Old South would never again flourish in this place. But to admit it — to themselves or anyone else — would have been disgrace, ultimate shame. The failure of the old way was not to be discussed or even mentioned. The culture covered over this looming reality, ignored it, denied it, primarily with alcohol. Booze flowed through plantation families like water. Every person was affected by it; every family struggled with it. But one did not acknowledge the reality of this great opiate either. The family drunk — there might actually be three or four — had to be masqueraded as an upstanding southern gentleman or lady. This was the game the community played.

I genuinely came to like and respect some people in Fayette. The county agent, Wilton, was a kindhearted man who spent his weekdays trying to assist the farmers of the region, white and black, in keeping acquainted with the most up-to-date information on growing their crops. Wilton's self-assigned mission in life was to help everyone; he spent his Saturdays running the local Boy Scout troop. He and I would often travel the dirt roads in his pickup truck, he visiting the farmers and I visiting the Presbyterians. There was a woman, very capable and educated, who devoted her life to trying to prop up and hold together three generations of alcoholic men in her family. She lived her life against great odds, but she never seemed to run out of hope. The bank president, a very kind and gentle man, maintained such high integrity and competence that the examiners rarely found anything to question. And there were others to be mentioned in the stories that follow.

Unfortunately, however, the reigning atmosphere in Fayette was established not by the people of strength and goodwill but by people afflicted with "Mississippi fever." It was not a time when we were going to be led in good directions. The folks who could have done so would have to wait for another era.

Union Church, seventeen miles to the east of Fayette, was totally different. No pretense whatever! It was a fork-in-the-road village of hardworking farmers whose last thought in life was to try to impress anyone. They couldn't have cared less what people thought.

Founded 150 years earlier by Scotch Presbyterians from North Carolina, Union Church still proliferated with Highland names: McCormick, McArn, McKell, Mateer, McKenzie, McCabe, McCord, and McArthur.

A woman in Edinburgh, Scotland, once said to me, "The Scots are a rather severe people," and this severity had certainly made its way across the ocean to Union Church. The community bore heavily the remnants of their demanding, Presbyterian past. Even the parts that had been dropped away over the years were still very much alive in memory.

I truly loved Union Church. I was myself barely a generation off a tobacco farm in North Carolina's Yadkin River Valley, my roots were Scottish, and I felt that the people of Union Church were my brothers and sisters. I talked their language and loved their food, never tired of their stories, and resonated with the rhythms of their farm life. I also liked their attitude toward the racial uproar that was sweeping the South: they had lived, worked, and played amid black people all their lives, and they saw no reason for either group to fear or hate the other.

The cause of civil rights was sweeping the nation. President Lyndon Johnson had proposed wide-ranging legislation to the U.S. Congress, and the 1964 Civil Rights Act would soon be law. Dr. Martin Luther King Jr. was the lead story on every television news program. Charles Evers had organized the majority black population of Adams County in a highly effective and crippling economic boycott of downtown Natchez, and he would soon move that boycott one county north to Fayette. Civil rights groups were holding demonstrations in towns all across the state, including ours.

Mississippi was a seething cauldron of hatred and violence, all of it tucked just beneath the surface of southern graciousness. In 1962, while waging an ultimately unsuccessful campaign to prevent the integration of the University of Mississippi, Governor Ross Barnett had declared, "We are facing the most critical hour in the history of our nation. We must either submit to the unlawful dictates of the federal government or stand up like men and tell them, 'Never!'" In the three-month period between June 15 and September 17, 1964, twenty-three black Mississippi churches were burned or bombed. Ku Klux Klan activity across the state had revived.

The *Jackson Clarion-Ledger,* the state's leading newspaper, played race-baiting games and touted communist conspiracy theories almost daily. Integrationist columnist Drew Pearson was printed on the editorial page as the liberal we loved most to hate. (It is significant that the

Clarion-Ledger would become one of the most professional, enlightened, and progressive newspapers in the South, winning a Pulitzer Prize in 1981 for its public service.)

Beneath Mississippi's hatred was a deep suspicion, distrust of anyone from outside, a profound dislike for new thoughts or ideas. As imported residents of Fayette, we never escaped the feeling that we were suspect. Especially while our car bore an out-of-state license plate, people who did not know us would stop, stare, and frown. Many of our own church members were willing to be cordial but not willing to let us make any real connection into their lives. It was a paranoia that afflicted the entire state.

Mississippi of 1964 was unending contradiction. Outwardly charming, gracious people; hatred and violence boiling just underneath. A legally dry state; alcohol everywhere. Fervent faith; rampant prejudice. Enormous wealth; widespread poverty. Fierce pride in the state colleges, especially Ole Miss, which sat atop the national football rankings; senators, congressmen, and newspaper editors who quietly sent their children to Vanderbilt, Duke, and the University of Virginia.

I went to Mississippi young and idealistic. I was fresh out of seminary, entering my first pastorate. My wife reminds me now that I was certain I could change the social attitudes of my entire congregation just by preaching the Bible. I was confident that if I spoke the Word, they would listen. It was a fine idea.

There were highly significant, native-born heroes in Mississippi, people of great courage, people whose conviction directly cut across the grain of popular opinion. The nation did not come to know these people. They were not folks the national media would ever meet on visits to the state. A few authors have talked about them, but mostly they are unknown. Our collective memory is poorer for it. I feel it a privilege to be able to tell a few of their stories.

The tales that follow come from Fayette and Union Church. Some tell of people with truly heroic character. Others tell of people less attractive. Set together, the paint the picture of southwest Mississippi in the mid–1960s.

Starters

The U.S. Post Office in Fayette was two blocks from our house. On our first visit, we were given keys to the pastor's mailbox. One of us would go there each morning to check for mail. As I left the post office one morning, I noticed that the trash can beside the front door — obviously placed there for junk mail — was full to overflowing with copies of a magazine. The container was jammed, and a stack was building on the floor. "Whatever magazine it is, it must be really unpopular here," I thought to myself. Picking one up, I saw that it was the *Presbyterian Survey*, published monthly by my denomination and sent free to every Presbyterian family. The *Survey*, amid its articles on theology and church events, was openly supporting civil rights. It had published a number of editorials over the past several years.

I realized that my church members, the people I would be preaching to and visiting, were voicing their total disdain by creating this stack. I saw a new face of what it would mean to be pastor of Fayette Presbyterian Church.

A year later, Nancy and I sent a contribution to Dr. Martin Luther King Jr's. Southern Christian Leadership

Conference. The SCLC then periodically sent us its literature. The mail clerks would simply look at me and shake their heads.

One of the things Nancy, as pastor's wife, was clearly expected to do in Fayette was attend Women of the Church meetings. Nancy was an educated woman with a sociology degree from the University of North Carolina, an abiding interest in diverse world cultures, a voracious appetite for reading newspapers and good books, and a well-developed talent for playing the piano. She also had a social conscience.

She characterized Fayette Women of the Church meetings as "tea sandwiches, flower arranging, gossip, and bridge" among a group of people who should have found something constructive to do with their lives. She came home from her first meeting reporting that one woman had said, "I think those three civil rights boys killed themselves. They were just trying to give Mississippi a bad name, trying to bring us negative publicity." There was general agreement with that idea. At the next meeting, a month later, Nancy wanted to ask, "Do you think those civil rights workers buried themselves in that dam?"

At times in Fayette Nancy and I would find ourselves suffocating in "segregation talk"—how cruelly the nation was persecuting Mississippi, how good we were to our "colored" people, how terrible the outside agitators were to try to change everything, how self-righteous and vilifying Attorney General Robert Kennedy was. Most folks seemed to agree that conversation like this was valid and correct. Segregation talk could happen in any conversation anywhere; it seemed to happen most often if we were captive in someone's home and couldn't walk away. A couple of hours of it would leave us weary and limp. Our heads would hurt, our muscles would feel tight, our faces would ache from trying to maintain plastic civility.

We soon, however, found a cure. We had taken with us to Mississippi Pete Seeger and Peter, Paul, and Mary record albums. Whenever the segregation talk had nearly numbed us, we would come home, lock all the doors of our house, close the windows, turn up the record player as loud as we could, and let Seeger sing, "If you miss me at the back of the bus..." throughout the house. We would sing along and dance. Then we'd play "We Shall Overcome," "Oh, Freedom," and "Blowin' in the Wind." It was marvelous recovery therapy, truly amazing how quickly we regained our perspective! We would wonder sometimes if anyone outside was listening, but in those moments it didn't seem to matter.

Next to the Presbyterian Church a man named Josef Schmidt operated a shop from which he would do repairs for people's homes. He came to turn on our water and gas just after we moved in. A tallish, slender man in his mid-fifties, Mr. Schmidt spoke with a touch of a German accent.

I noticed that he always wore a large campaign-style button on his shirt. The button proclaimed, in bold, black letters on a white background, "NEVER!" repeating Governor Barnett's rally cry. I did not see anyone else wearing a similar button. I thought to myself that Mr. Schmidt must be pretty rabid, but he never brought up the subject.

I did fall into a longer conversation with him one day. He told me about his life. His father had moved from

Germany to America just after the turn of the century, settling in a small town in Minnesota. Mr. Schmidt had been young, he said, when his family had faced the enormous difficulty of being recently arrived German Americans. World War I had broken out, and in his town that had made anyone with a recent German history suspect. He told stories of how his family had been derided and mocked, how he and his sister had been picked on mercilessly at school, how his father's business has been torched and nearly destroyed, how his family had spent sleepless nights guarding their house. These childhood experiences had obviously left indelible marks on this poor man's memory. The family members had tried their best to convince the town that they were now Americans. They had flown an American flag. They had even tried to change their name from Schmidt to Smith. But they could not lose their accents. As long as World War I continued, people had refused to stop being suspicious and mean. Only years after the war had ended did the Schmidts finally outlive the stigma. Mr. Schmidt put deep feeling into the stories as he told them.

I realized that his "NEVER!" button said two things. first, it proclaimed that he was dead-set opposed to racial integration, that "NEVER!" should we allow blacks to eat at our lunch tables and marry our daughters. But even more loudly it proclaimed, "Please accept me! I desperately want to be one with you! I don't want to endure any more persecution!"

It was very sad. To try to gain the community's acceptance, this man was willing to wage the same vicious attack against other people that he had hated so much when it was waged against him. Having been a victim in no way made him identify with the victim's cause. "NEVER!"

was his way to social acceptance. I felt sorry for the fear in which he had lived his life.

Beyond that button, I always found Mr. Schmidt to be a very nice and caring man.

Mr. Cecil's World

I began hearing about "Mr. Cecil" as soon as I arrived in Fayette. "A one-of-a-kind person," one church member described him. "Truly unique," said another. "Sort of the town eccentric, in his own brilliant way," said a third.

Mr. Cecil was a spry old gentleman several years beyond retirement. He lived with his wife in a very nice though not lavish house. He possessed a kind of dapper elegance through which he conveyed his natural southern grace: you knew immediately and without question that you were going to like him. He was one of the regulars on the plantation party circuit—fully a part of local society—but his thought world came from somewhere else. The things Mr. Cecil enjoyed talking about with me and the things everyone else in town regularly talked about bore very little in common. I think he nurtured within himself a large private world into which few people were ever invited. I felt honored to have received an invitation.

The first time I visited him, I was ushered into his reading room by his maid. On his coffee table lay the *Jackson Clarion-Ledger,* the *Atlanta Constitution,* the *Washington Post,* and the *New York Times. Harpers, Atlantic Monthly,* and *Newsweek* were there also, plus several books. The bookshelves around him were packed. The room resembled a well-appointed professor's office.

"A fine sermon yesterday," he said as he greeted me. I had preached on the "beast within," quoting William

Golding, John Howard Griffin, and others. We discussed parallels in other literature—the theme was certainly not new.

Then we moved to other subjects: President Johnson's war on poverty; Barry Goldwater, who would soon become the Republican nominee for president; the ever-expanding Vietnam War; the anticommunist fever that continued to pervade the country. On every subject Mr. Cecil displayed extensive knowledge and a much different mind-set from what I usually found in Fayette. I was fascinated. I found myself already looking forward to future conversations.

At length, we came to race. I couldn't believe my ears! "Fayette faces extinction if we don't change!" he said in a kind of low, definite tone. "Given what is happening across the world, there is no way we can maintain the past. It's dead! The entire flow is in another direction. The black man in this country is going to gain his rightful position beside the rest of us, and no amount of Mississippi resistance will stop it. Our governor can block the university admissions building day and night, but it won't change what's coming.

"Besides, it's the only right thing to do. Segregation is wrong, wrong by every measure of justice known to humanity. Clearly wrong by Christian principles. There is no way you can justify having one man rule another.

"I love the people in Fayette. They are my kin, my best friends, wonderful folks. But we're all living in the final stage of a make-believe world. I don't know when it will change, but it can't be long."

"You really think segregation is wrong, Mr. Cecil?" I asked.

"Oh, I most certainly do," he replied. "And so do you! You haven't been here long, but your sermons are transparent. You aren't saying it openly, because you want to keep your job for a while. But you know as well as I do what is right." He read me accurately.

Mr. Cecil had taught history in the local high school. He was remembered for his broad-ranging knowledge of the past and for the stories he generated. According to one story, he had been the high school football coach for several years. He had not been a particularly successful coach, but neither was anyone else in Fayette. At a crucial moment in one game, however, the Fayette quarterback had called time-out and had come running to the sideline. He asked Mr. Cecil what play he should call. Mr. Cecil was said to have replied, "My lands, son, if you can't figure out what play to call, you have no business being my quarterback," and to have sent the youngster back into the game.

Mr. Cecil shared one piece of wisdom that I still remember. "The state of Mississippi does one thing entirely right," he said, "and that is alcohol. You won't find a better alcohol policy anywhere!

"The whole state is legally dry. There's not a drop of permissible alcohol anywhere. It's all banned! Zero, everywhere! That makes the Baptists, who outnumber everyone else by far, exceedingly happy: they live in a dry state.

"You can find alcohol anywhere you go — in grocery stores, in cafes, in roadhouses, at parties, in private homes! Anyone who wants booze can locate it readily. That makes all the social people happy. They can party to their hearts' content.

"The Mississippi state legislature levies what is officially called the 'bootleg liquor tax,' a tax collected by every sheriff. It's on the law books: the bootleg liquor tax; you can look it up yourself. The dealers willingly pay it because they'd rather do that than have prohibition hung around their necks. That tax keeps the politicians happy because they get their money.

"Can you think of a system better designed to make everyone happy? The Baptists, the socialites, and the politicians. It's pure genius. Saves a lot of controversy. I don't know why every state in the South doesn't do the same thing!"

We chuckled together over the absurdity of it all.

A Short Sermon by Mr. Bunt

The Reverend Mr. Matthew Bunt had, I was told, spent his career as a missionary in Africa. A dedicated servant of the Lord, Mr. Bunt had labored for years carrying the gospel to the villages of his region. He was described to me as a man of rigorous belief, conservative mentality, and serious intention, a gentleman of the finest sort.

He had now grown old. He was thin and gray, but he was still a formidable presence. Perhaps it was his look of resolution that made you sense as he stood to speak that the moments that followed would be significant.

For several years, since his retirement from the mission field, Mr. Bunt had served the Presbyterian Church in a small community near the eastern border of Mississippi, his home. How long he stayed there I do not know. I never had the opportunity to meet him in person, but because of a single five-minute experience, one short sermon, he has been a companion of mine ever since.

It was a cool fall day. I had been in Mississippi only a few weeks and was still very new to how things happened there. South Mississippi Presbytery, which consisted of commissioners from every Presbyterian church in the southern third of the state, was meeting in Hattiesburg. With the civil rights movement in full motion around us, someone had presented a resolution proposing that we declare publicly that our churches were open to all people regardless of race or color, that we did not intend to discriminate against anyone. Some commissioners would greatly favor this resolution; others would strongly oppose it. The debate was certain to occupy at least two hours.

Those who offered the resolution — most of them young people like me — spoke in support. "God wills unity, not division," said one. "God breaks down dividing walls of hostility," said another, referring to Paul's letter to the Ephesians in the Bible. "God builds bridges, not chasms." "God alone is to decide who enters the doors of a church, not us."

Some eloquent statements were made. I realized that the progressives had had a fair bit of practice by now and were beginning to be pretty good.

There were also the negatives, the full range.

"Why would God have created different nations if God wanted them all mixed together. This would go against the natural order of the universe."

"You can't legislate morality. New laws don't create new hearts. God creates new hearts. Our job is to lead people to God, not to pass laws. If we start legislating, we are putting ourselves in the place of God. That is blasphemy."

"God told Adam and Eve to fill the earth and subdue it, not to integrate it."

"We know the Mississippi Negroes. They wouldn't be happy in our churches. They need their own churches, where they can worship their way. Their way is different from our way. It won't work to have us all together."

"The only Negroes who are going to come to our churches are the rabble-rousers, the ones demonstrating. They don't want to worship; they just want to disturb everyone else. It would upset the sincere devotion of true Christian people if we let them in."

"If God wanted Negroes and whites to intermingle, why did God create redbirds and bluebirds? Watch the bird feeder outside your window some morning. Even those little creatures know better than to integrate. We should know better, too."

"It all started in Moscow! The communists are set on wrecking our southern way of life! Lenin said it first, then Stalin: 'All we got to do is attack their moral character, and the best way to do that is mix them all together.' It comes directly from Khrushchev and his crowd. They have promised to destroy us. They have said they will make us the dirt under their feet. And since they can't do it by military power, they will do it by undermining our moral fiber. Just read the House Un-American Activity Committee reports! See for yourself! Then you won't have any doubt what this movement is about. Integration is Red through and through! It stinks a heavy Kremlin odor. Our job is to protect the ways of God against evil."

My idealism took a giant leap toward reality that day. I had read about opinions like these, but I had never heard them spoken in person. Here were successful, intelligent human beings saying they believed these things. I sat in stunned disbelief. From that point forward in my life, I realized that self-justification is far stronger in us than reason, that when we feel we need to vindicate ourselves, we can resort to nearly anything.

After the debate had gone on for a while, a frail, gray man rose to his feet on the other side of the room from me. "Who is that?" I asked the friend beside me.

"The Reverend Mr. Matthew Bunt," he replied, and he gave me the rundown on Mr. Bunt. We both sat fearing the worst. We shouldn't have.

"If we tell Negro people they are not welcome in our worship," this little man roared, "then my decades of missionary labor in West Africa have been a sham! If we tell them that we want them to be Christians, but not in our congregations, then I have been preaching a divided Christ. For years I have labored among Negroes. They are as good as I am, as bad as I am. God loves them the same way God loves me. In Africa I have made dear friends, people I will cherish as long as I live.

"A Negro man risked his life for me. I was in danger of being attacked by a snake. That snake could have killed me. My Negro friend, with enormous courage, broke the snake's back. He could have been seriously injured himself. I owe my life to that man.

"The last thing I said to him before I left Africa was, 'Come to see me in Mississippi.' If he comes, can I not bring him to my church? Can I not offer to him the same hand of Christian fellowship he offered me?"

The elders who were attending the meeting from Mr. Bunt's congregation sat in frozen silence. They loved the old man, respected him, would not cross him, but they most certainly did not agree with what he was saying now, and they did not want to be publicly associated with his position. No one openly dissented, but neither did they smile or nod. Mr. Bunt was making this speech alone.

"As you decide how you will vote here today," Mr. Bunt continued, "I ask you to think of the message you will send to the world. The world is not just the space between Alabama and Louisiana, not just these Mississippi fields. The world has as many dark-skinned Christians as light-skinned Christians. Do we really want to draw a dividing line through the middle here today? Do we really wish to proclaim that God has called two churches, one for us and the other for everyone else?

"I was born in Mississippi, raised in Mississippi, educated in Mississippi. I love Mississippi. I will die in Mississippi. But Mississippi is not the universe. We are part of a bigger humanity, part of God's whole creation. I ask you not to vote today to wall yourself off, not to act as if Mississippi needs to be protected from the rest of the world. I ask you to join arms with your faithful brothers and sisters everywhere in proclaiming Jesus Christ. That is the only way our message will preach God's word!"

Reverberating through the assembly, Mr. Bunt's final words evoked thunderous silence. Not a sound! Dead still. No one dared even a murmur.

Mr. Bunt sat down. His elders looked to the side as if nothing at all had happened. The debate was over. Even the moderator did not move swiftly to continue the meeting.

The vote went two to one against the motion, in favor of keeping our churches segregated. Mr. Bunt had lost. His persuasion had not been sufficient. The wall of prejudice remained. There was, however, no rejoicing and no self-congratulating among the victors, as there often was. The great beast had sustained a powerful blow. Mr. Bunt had not really lost at all.

I am sure Mr. Bunt is now dead. I wish I could place a memorial wreath on his grave. Many times his presence has walked through my life, telling me what I must do, giving me encouragement. There come moments when it is necessary for us to stand before a truly disagreeing, hostile audience and speak what we believe, not because it will prevail but because it is right. It can happen in a large meeting; it can happen in a small conversation among two or three. Simply to proclaim the message is victory; silence is defeat. If we are timid and keep quiet, if our lives are ruled by fear, we may as well not exist. Fear never gives victory a chance. Conviction, clearly stated, calls forth a response, a decision, from other people, and often bears consequences we could never predict.

I still recall him. He is dead, but he lives. I wish he could know the effect his speech had on me. Maybe he does know. I continue to thank him for his short sermon that shaped the rest of my life.

Standing on Holy Ground

I had been in Fayette nearly a year before I met Albert, who was to become a close and dear friend. I first discovered him in a chance conversation in the Ford dealership that he owned and operated. I had gone into the dealership to buy an auto part, and I overheard him talking about the civil rights march scheduled for our main street a few days later. I wondered from the few words I picked up if he were of a different mind-set from most of Fayette. Not wanting to let the possibility pass, I introduced myself. "Yes, I know you," he said, "Mary and I attended Marie McLaurin's wedding in your church, and you live just up the street from us." I asked him about his civil rights remarks and quickly learned that I had discovered a jewel.

Albert had grown up in Hermanville, Mississippi, which was about as big as it sounds. He had reached adulthood during the depression and had eventually started the Fayette Ford dealership. He was definitely cut from a different piece of cloth from most of his neighbors. I asked him how he got to be that way, and he would only comment that he had attended college out of state. I suspected there was more.

Albert believed that it was wrong that 80 percent of the eligible voters in the county had never been allowed to register to vote and that the voting registrar had declared publicly that the first black who tried would end up dead on the sidewalk in front of the county courthouse. Albert believed that it was wrong that a highly disproportionate share of the county's tax money went to the smaller of two separate and very unequal public schools. Albert believed that it was wrong that it was virtually impossible for a white person to be convicted of a crime against a black and equally impossible for a black person to be acquitted of a crime against a white. Albert believed that it was wrong that the town government maintained two Little League baseball fields, one beautifully manicured with chain-link fences, field lights, a press box, and a public-address system, and the other a literal weed patch with stumps, briars, and not even a backstop behind home plate.

Albert was both a very humble and a very forthright man. For thirty years he had quietly but firmly voiced his beliefs: among the town's business owners, of which he was one, in the town council, on the governing board of his Methodist church, in casual conversation. His message was singular: "Friends, if we don't make things right in our town, then one of these days the federal government is going to come in here and make them right for us, and we will all wish we had done it for ourselves."

I remember a Kiwanis Club meeting held in the town restaurant. I was Albert's guest. The speaker was an executive in an area utility company. He gave a fairly typical speech, exposing communist influence at various levels of the federal government and branding the civil rights movement a Kremlin plot to subvert traditional southern virtue. On finishing, he received enthusiastic applause, the room erupting in congratulation. As the applause stopped, however, Albert rose to his feet. He spoke in his humble but forthright way: "Sir, I mean no disrespect for you or your office, and I certainly do not hold malice toward any of the people in this room, because they are all my friends. But I have to disagree with many of the things you have just said." He went on briefly to state his own case in behalf of justice and fairness for all people.

I also one day walked into a conversation on the sidewalk in front of the hardware store. Several friends were gathered, and Albert was obviously replying to what someone else had said. "Well, the way I look at it, they've got a right to complain. They clean our houses, cook our food, raise our children, carry our loads, empty our trash cans. And yet all the money belongs to us. They never get but a few dollars. They have to live off what the federal government sends them. We talk about how lazy and no good and worthless they are and how all they do is depend on someone to take care of them. But it seems like to me that the problem is with us as much as it is with them."

"Albert, you been talking that line for years, and you haven't convinced anyone yet," one friend replied in a kind of joshing rebuff. Albert had grown accustomed to being ignored.

One morning as I walked the two blocks to downtown to get the mail, I heard the news that there had been trouble at Albert's Ford place during the night. I inquired and found out the story. The Ku Klux Klan had had a rally out in a field somewhere. The members had listened to some rousing speeches, put a few beers under their belts, and then decided that they were ready to persecute their favorite villain. On previous occasions, they had broken glass and cut tires on Albert's used cars. This time, they had thrown rocks through the huge front window of his dealership and set several of his used cars on fire. His car lot was a charred mess when I got there, the penetrating odor of soot hanging everywhere.

Albert, visibly upset but still in control of himself, told me what had happened. The town's one policeman had called him about 3:00 A.M., and the volunteer fire department had been dispatched, so that everyone knew by now.

"What does this do to you?" I asked. I wondered, frankly, if it would cause him to shut down his dealership and move to another town. I would not have blamed him. These things were especially hard on his wife.

"I've gotten so used to things like this that it doesn't do much of anything to me any longer," he replied. "The only thing that worries me is that the insurance company is threatening to cut me off. I don't even report little incidents like this now, because I need to keep my insurance in case something really big happens."

"What will you do if they cut you off?" I asked.

I expected him to say, "I guess I'll have to learn to be quieter about what I believe."

Instead, Albert, rather matter-of-factly, spoke words that are still distinctly etched on my memory: "Oh, I'll just have to operate my business without insurance."

"You mean it wouldn't change the things you stand for?"

"Oh, no, I'd never even consider that," he said, wavering none at all. I knew at that moment that I was standing on holy ground.

Albert would never be blessed with the biggest Ford dealership south of Nashville. He would never be granted an award for distinguished service by the president of the United States. He would never be featured on the national television news or make the cover of *Time* magazine. He would not be voted outstanding layman in his

Methodist church. And he would not even occupy a couple of pages in someone's book until much, much later.

But Albert's life was poetry — clear, simple truth amid a great system of fabrication and falsehood, a clarion call to the faint of heart, a sign showing how to build the future. The gift Albert offered was strength of conviction, something found not often in our play-it-safe world. No greater gift can one life give to another.

The Jefferson County Boycott

Charles Evers was the older brother of Medgar Evers, a leader of the National Association for the Advancement of Colored People who had been brutally slain in front of his home in Jackson on June 12, 1963. In 1965, Charles Evers organized the black residents of Natchez, twenty miles south of Fayette, and spent several months boycotting white-owned businesses because of their unwillingness to hire black people. The boycott had been extremely effective. Evers had been able to marshal nearly 100 percent cooperation from blacks, and the stores of Natchez and Adams County had nearly suffocated. The town fathers — definitely all male — had finally negotiated a settlement that essentially capitulated to every demand on Evers's list. It was a major victory for the black community, certainly for their economic situation but even more for their pride. Yes, they, with their superior numbers, could stand up against oppressive white racism and prevail. It was a revolution in self-esteem.

Having won this battle, Evers moved one county up the Mississippi River to Fayette and Jefferson County, 80 percent of whose nine thousand residents were black, an even higher percentage than in Adams. Here Evers could win more than a skirmish. He could gain control of county politics; become mayor of Fayette, with the capacity to attract large sums of federal dollars; and make the town his operating base for years to come.

Only weeks earlier, the Jefferson County voting rolls had been completely transformed. On a Monday morning federal marshals had presented themselves in the office of the Jefferson County voting registrar and announced that they were there to implement the new federal voting rights act.

The racial segregation of voter registration in Jefferson County had previously been rigid and thorough. Not since the 1870s had any black person been registered. Vivid, memorable stories circulated of the threats and intimidation that had resulted when three black people once tried to register to vote. The registrar, it was said, had stormed out of his office, ranting, raving, cursing, and declared publicly that, "The next damned nigger that walks up to that door will end up dead on the sidewalk!" The registrar's personality was such that he was probably speaking the truth.

Under Mississippi law, anyone, white or black, who moved into the county faced a two-year waiting period for voter registration. There was also a preregistration test that consisted of whatever questions the registrar wanted to ask. Any answer he did not like caused failure.

On that Monday morning, however, federal marshals commandeered the registrar's office. For all his previous threats and venom, all he could do was sit behind his desk and watch. The line of registrants formed early and lasted until late afternoon. In about three days there were twice as many blacks registered to vote as there had been whites. This week, more than any other, changed the history of Fayette.

With the voting rolls now majority black, Evers's people moved in. They came quietly at first, without fanfare.

They met black residents mostly in churches. They talked about the Adams County victory and how the same thing could happen in Fayette. The boycott they proposed would call for no more buying in any store owned by a white.

During these organizational days, I saw the anxiety growing in the white community. There was a collective sense that huge things were happening just beneath the surface—a whale swimming under the boat—but among those accustomed to controlling things, no one had any idea how to regulate this. The tension mounted.

White people began telling stories about threats Evers was supposedly using to scare blacks into honoring the boycott—the threat of cutting off their welfare, of ostracism, of whipping. The whites of Fayette suddenly took on a concern for the fair treatment and safety of blacks that I had never heard before. The stories of how much they were in danger from the threats of this outside agitator grew with the tension.

Finally, boycott day came, just before Christmas. It was amazing. After an initial demonstration in downtown Fayette to state publicly what they were doing, seven thousand black people simply disappeared. None were to be found anywhere. The sidewalks were empty. The stores were quiet. The streets were bare. They were gone.

The county's twenty-four hundred white customers made barely a ripple at the cash registers. At first the white community played down the effect. "It's not hurting us," the hardware store owner told me. "They never bought anything anyway." "They'll be back as soon as they get hungry," the grocery store owner said. "We are the only food store in the county that advances the credit they all need. Just wait."

That first week the community newspaper, the *Fayette Chronicle,* printed not a single word acknowledging the boycott, as if it didn't exist. This was, I realized, a game at which white folks had had plenty of practice. Soon, however, the empty cash registers could no longer be ignored. The bills came due and the money to pay them had not come in. At this moment, the town became aware of how dependent all of us were on those welfare checks. Without federal aid, there was no white prosperity either.

The challenge was struck! "We'll beat'um!" our community declared. "We'll kill this boycott, and they'll wish they had never heard of Charles Evers." We had learned nothing from Natchez. Downtown conversation became strongly confrontational, focusing on the evils of the Evers movement. He was funded, it was said, by rich easterners trying to kill off business competition from the South. Its leaders had been trained at an eastern Tennessee communist training center led by Myles Horton, the same facility where Martin Luther King had spent so much time and where Rosa Parks had attended a workshop two weeks before she refused to take a backseat on a Montgomery bus. The movement was antifamily, anti-American, antichurch, and anti-God. The federal government wanted to drive down all the white people and give the South to the Negroes. "Little brother Bobby" (Attorney General Robert Kennedy) was the leader of it all.

I was amazed at how completely and effectively we could deny that the main cause of the boycott was our own racism.

In his biography, *Have No Fear: A Black Man's Fight for Respect in America* (New York: John Wiley, 1997), Evers said of these events, "Once we had a voting majority in Fayette, we sprung a boycott. I'd just got concessions in Natchez . . . and [we] asked for nineteen concessions in Fayette. Hire more Negroes in stores and on the town's payroll. Integrate stores and restaurants. Call us 'sir' and 'ma'am.' The whites balked, so [we] . . . called a Christmas boycott in Fayette" (202).

One Saturday morning, members of the Americans for the Preservation of the White Race (APWR) arrived en masse from various parts of Mississippi. I remember in particular two vans parked near our house with large lettering on the side, "White Knights of the Green Forest, Tupelo, Mississippi," obviously a Klan chapter. Welcomed by an entire entourage of town officials, APWR people circulated through the Main Street stores, buying dry goods, hardware, drug items, plumbing supplies, and food — filling their trucks and vans with orders to carry back home. "The cash registers were dancing!" the *Fayette Chronicle* proclaimed the following week.

Around 11:00 A.M., the Klan gathered on the courthouse steps in full regalia: white robes adorned with large crosses, white hoods, and white dunce hats. (I have never to this day been able to avoid my own feeling of anger when someone co-opts the primary Christian symbol of God's love, the cross, to convey prejudice, division, and hatred.) The Klan members lined up on the courthouse steps in formation. First they unveiled a Klan flag and a rebel flag. Then they recited something that sounded like a pledge of allegiance to a white supremacist America.

Then the comments began: a government plot to undermine our southern way of life, a movement led by the Antichrist to replace Christianity with godless communism, a program to have all our daughters marrying field hands. The longer they stood there, the more uncomfortable and ridiculous they looked. Several had to fall out of formation to get water or go to the bathroom. They all sweated and sweltered.

Finally the group's leader made his auspicious appearance. He delivered a fiery speech full of accusation and racist bigotry. "A separated America, that's what we need," he proclaimed, "where the good, decent, hardworking, right-living Christians can live on one side, and the lazy, degenerate, pervert communists on the other. Race-mixing will be the death of America." I could not imagine how any member of the human family could welcome his venom.

But the crowd cheered—cheered the ideology, cheered the bursts of enthusiasm, cheered the slurs against Charles Evers and other blacks. The demonstration mercifully broke up shortly after noon so that all the participants could travel back to their homes in time for Sunday school the next morning.

The APWR's Saturday visits became a frequent ritual for Fayette. Additional people came. The newspaper hailed them as our "savior-brothers," extolling the state for its solidarity.

The official word in the town and in the newspaper was that those weekly spending sprees were more than offsetting the boycott, that Fayette's merchants were prospering splendidly. But every store owner knew better. The visits represented hardly a blip, a 5 percent improvement at best when more than 50 percent had been lost.

In his biography, Evers said, "The Klan drove into town with Confederate flags on their cars and staged a big 'buy-in' in Fayette to help the white racist merchants. But whether by meanness or plain stupidity, they passed the merchants a big load of bad checks. So we got the last laugh. Our boycott cost the town lots of money, and many whites in Fayette never forgave us" (202).

It was during this time that my church elders decided that we needed a worship attendance policy in case "some of the civil rights people decided to walk in on us some Sunday morning." My governing board and I had an earnest, if heavily tilted, debate. "If they were coming to worship, it might be different. But the fact is they won't come to do anything but stir people up," my elders said. "We need to instruct the ushers to tell them they are not welcome." My position was, "If anyone is turned away from the worship of this church on a Sunday morning, there will be no worship for any of us that day. We will simply shut down the service and go home. Either everyone is welcome in God's house, or no one is welcome."

The vote went five to zero—I voted only if it was needed to break a tie. The next Sunday, worship attendance dropped from thirty-eight to twelve, and it remained at twelve for the rest of my time in Fayette.

After a number of weeks of the strangling boycott, the local merchants finally sought negotiation. One of my church elders, the young grocery store owner, invited me to attend the first negotiation with him. He and I had remained jovial and mutually respectful despite our strongly different views. (He actually almost seemed to take an odd pride in me.)

The negotiation took place in the basement of the town hall. About sixteen businessmen, at least half of them my church members, seated themselves in three rows of chairs facing a table. Precisely at the hour set for the negotiation, Evers appeared. It was the first time virtually any of us had seen him; he had previously remained a silent but powerful figure in the background. He marched into the room by himself, erect and confident in a well-tailored business suit, and seated himself at the table. The effect was stunning. It was apparent that he needed no assistance whatever and that he was there to do serious business.

He announced, "Gentlemen, we are here to see if we can negotiate an end to the economic boycott of Jefferson County. If it is your wish to end this boycott, we can do it. If it is not your wish, then the boycott will go on indefinitely. What happens lies in your hands." Evers then went on to list his demands: black workers in the stores, black workers in the town offices, a black police officer, respect for black people.

When he stopped, he waited for someone to reply. The first person on his feet was the young town dentist, referred to locally as "Doc." Doc was not from Fayette. He had graduated from dental school only shortly before and was obviously paying off his dental school loan by serving in a rural location. Doc clutched in his hands a manila folder full of papers. He began asking questions from the papers: "Mr. Evers, according to a U.S. Senate Committee's research, three members of your Natchez staff received training from a proven communist agent" (he named the staff members and the agent). "This training was in tactics for overthrowing the U.S. Government. Can you deny to us that this happened?"

There was a collective groan across the room, the first time I had heard this response to the communism line. The line had always played well before, but I sensed that, even in Fayette, we had now reached the limit. Another man stood and said, "Doc, all that communism stuff is well and good in its place, but that's not what we're here to talk about right now. We're here to settle a boycott, and we need you to put that file back in your drawer and save it."

Doc was wounded. Mortally hurt. He thought he was doing the community a favor, providing specifics for the charges against Evers's group. He protested mildly, "But this is important! Just let me ask a few questions."

"It may be important to you, Doc, but it's not important to us. Sit down and put that stuff away, and let's see if we can make some progress. We're here because we need to settle this boycott, not to rant and rave about communism." Doc sat down, mortified.

At that moment I understood clearly that the businessmen of Jefferson County had moved from blind opposition to grudging respect for Charles Evers. They had come to understand that they were dealing with a tough-minded, hard-fisted business negotiator of their own ilk, not a submissive nobody who would buckle at the first threat. They knew how to play hardball. They had been doing business that way all their lives. And they actually found pleasure in it, even though they knew down deep that they were going to lose.

About two days later I was in the grocery store. The young owner smiled at me and said with obvious pride, "Hey, Jim, I talked to the big man today." The "big man" was Evers. I never thought I would hear that comment from a Fayette white.

After several weeks, an end to the boycott was negotiated, just as it had been in Natchez. In 1969, three years later, Evers would be elected mayor of Fayette.

In his 1971 autobiography, *Evers* (New York: World Publishing), Charles Evers wrote a letter to his murdered brother, Medgar:

> Your big brother is [now] the Mayor of Fayette. Imagine, Medgar, we black folks actually control and govern and live happily in a bi-racial town in the State of Mississippi. And it's your example that's steering us right: playing fair with one and all, white and black. I've learned how important it is for the community leader to crack down whenever bigotry and bullying occur. I'm as firm with my folks as Daddy was with us. In Fayette, you'll see something different in the people, something perky in the way they look at you, a kind of energy in their stride. The old hang-

dog look has gone. Now you see hope, you see friendliness, you see enthusiasm.

Remember, Medgar, when that old [Mississippi Governor] Bilbo warned that rabble [that] if they weren't careful they'd wake up to find those two little nigger boys [Medgar and Charles Evers], representing them? Well, he wasn't far wrong. We are representing them, quite a few of them. And the craziest thing of all, Medgar, is that now that they know us they kind of like us. (195–96)

Barbershop

There was a very popular barbershop in the tiny community of Lorman, six miles up the highway from Fayette. The shop was located beside the main highway in a concrete-block building painted white. A small barber pole attached to the corner announced the building's identity; the spiral stripes rotated when someone remembered to plug it in. Usually there were three barbers, on Saturday four. It was a community gathering spot for everyone from the bank president to the local construction workers.

As I sat in the barber chair one day, the customer in the chair next to me related to virtually everyone in the shop several salty tales from his experience as a construction worker on the Mississippi Gulf Coast. He obviously loved telling stories and wasn't about to miss an audience this good. His stories, aside from their natural bawdiness, were liberally punctuated with expletives, an array of cuss words that seemed to come quite naturally to him. There was nothing overly crude, nothing we all hadn't heard many times before, but the sum total was becoming a bit heavy.

The barber cutting my hair, the shop owner, grew increasing uneasy. He fidgeted this way and that, obviously in a dilemma. After several minutes, he finally turned to the man and said: "Hey, buddy, you don't want to talk that way in front of a preacher, do you?"

In one instant, a blanket of suffocating reverence settled over the entire barbershop, sterilizing the atmosphere. No one dared say anything without carefully thinking about it first, which meant that no one said anything.

I understood completely in that moment how my ordination had set me apart from the rest of humanity, placing me in a category of "different," making me a walking judgment against authenticity, a person from whom you needed to hide a piece of your natural self. "The preacher!"—more than once I have heard that warning whispered as I entered a room, and immediately the conversations have veered. For many years it bothered me; I wanted to be a regular guy like everyone else. I am no longer bothered: given the things some people talk about, I don't mind possessing the power to shut them up.

I had a friend in seminary who nearly got himself drummed out of the ministry because he insisted on greeting his church members in a small Shenandoah Valley town with "How the hell are you?" It was his rather pathetic effort to be one of them, and it violated every sensibility they possessed.

After several minutes of recovery time, the mood in the barbershop returned toward normal, and individual conversations were able to resume. My own barber started telling me about the automobile he had bought earlier that year. He loved it—automatic transmission (still an extra in 1965), 340 horsepower, fire-engine red, beige alpaca seat covers (imitation, of course), air-conditioning.

And then, with that special "male thing" gleam in his eye, he confided, "It has a guarantee of five years or fifty thousand miles. I drive a lot—eight thousand miles in the first six months—so I crawled under the hood and disconnected the odometer cable to keep the mileage reading from running up too fast." He seemed highly satisfied with his accomplishment, a private pride radiating from within.

I sat in that barber chair pondering the contradiction: "This man feels terribly guilty about my hearing cursing in his barbershop, but he does not feel the least bit guilty about telling me that he is in the process of swindling General Motors."

Strange ethics we human beings develop! I once knew a man who worried considerably that he might go to hell for playing an occasional golf game on Sunday morning but wasn't at all concerned that, though married, he was having affairs with two other women.

While I was in North Carolina, the largest religious body in the state spent four days of its annual convention debating whether the students on its college campuses should be allowed to dance. At the same time, students from North Carolina A& T in Greensboro were beginning sit-in demonstrations at the Woolworth's lunch counter.

The easiest thing to miss in life can be the main point.

I liked my barber and continued to go to him to get my hair cut.

The Shedrick Conspiracy

Shedrick was the big, middle-aged black man who worked at the funeral home next door to where we lived. The funeral home was owned and operated by a member of my church, Joe. Shedrick was likable, easy to get along with, and laid back. He nevertheless seemed to be everywhere: mowing the yard, pruning the bushes, painting the building, sweeping the porch, repairing the roof, waxing the vehicles, unloading the delivery trucks. I fell into the habit, when I was outdoors, of passing conversation with Shedrick. He was an enjoyable guy.

When I had come to Fayette from the seminary, I had brought two suits of clothes I had found in the seminary "mission closet." Some well-to-do Presbyterian about my size had died somewhere, and his estate had sent this pair of very nice suits to help needy students and fur-loughed missionaries. They were far better than any-thing I myself would have purchased. When I arrived in Fayette, however, I discovered to my disappointment that the deceased had been not quite as tall and several pounds heavier than I was. They really didn't fit. So I be-gan a quiet search for someone they would fit. It occurred to me one day that Shedrick might be the man.

I invited him into our living room one morning to look at the suits. To my—and his—delight, they fitted per-fectly. He looked elegant. I told him they were his. He voiced quietly, "I've never had anything like this before." Neither had I.

This was only the beginning. In the months ahead, people in my church, seeking to be nice to their pastor, brought us tons of food from their gardens: tomatoes, cucumbers, corn, squash, turnips, beets, okra. Summer-time created a farmers' market on our back porch. One man went fishing every week and would bring us twelve or fifteen bluegill with their mournful little eyes gazing up at us out of the ice bucket. Another man gave us a side of venison. I began quietly passing 80 percent of the food to Shedrick, simply because we couldn't eat it all. I told him, "Shedrick, you and your wife and seven kids can eat like royalty as long as you keep quiet. You could ruin me with a single murmur."

He had replied, "Reverend Jim, you'd be surprised at some of the things I know how to keep quiet about." I did not learn the full meaning of that remark until later.

One Saturday afternoon I was working in the backyard. The funeral home seemed quiet until I saw the back door open and Shedrick appear on the back porch. He sat on the steps to smoke a cigarette.

"Shedrick, you're working long hours this week," I said to him.

"Yeah," he replied, "we got a viewing tomorrow, and I'm getting things ready."

"Do you mean that in addition to everything else, you also prepare bodies?"

"Well, yeah," he said, blushing slightly, "I do that, too."

"I thought Joe would take care of that," I said.

"Everyone else thinks that too, "Shedrick replied, "but, naw, Mr. Joe, he don't really do very much here, just stays in charge of things. I prepare the bodies, wash them, embalm them, put the make-up on, dress them. I been doing it for years."

He paused. "Reverend, the white folks in this town would have a conniption if they knew a black man was fixing up their dead. They'd start imagining all kinds of stuff, building up their suspicions and stories. And pretty soon we'd have the biggest uproar you ever saw. Just as well if you keep this one quiet for me. Will you do that?" My mind reeled at the possibilities!

"Shedrick," I replied, "you'd be surprised at some of the things I know how to keep quiet about."

"I guess we could both ruin each other," he said.

"A conspiracy of silence, Shedrick," I replied.

He smiled and shook my hand.

What No One Ever Knew

In Fayette there was a man named Frank who owned the electronic appliance and repair store, the only one. Frank sold an assortment of clothes washers, dryers, dishwashers, radios, television sets, irons, toasters, and ranges—not a huge selection, but enough to keep people from having to drive to Natchez or Jackson when they wanted something.

Frank was a short man with a graying crew cut and stubby features. A bit soft-spoken and laid back, he was not at all the high-pressure appliance salesman typical of the larger markets. Frank just quietly ran a quality little store and let Fayette come to him.

He and his wife were members of my church and attended worship every Sunday, always sitting in the same seats and always bearing the same attentive looks. Despite their regularity, they seemed a bit off to the side of the community, not in the mainstream of the Fayette social network. They were not associated with the garden club, the Rotary Club, or the party circuit. They were cordial and apparently well liked among their church friends but seemed perfectly content to live on the periphery.

One day I went into Frank's store. I was searching for an electronic connector for our television set, trying to install a higher antenna that would pull in the Jackson stations better. I had asked Frank the previous Sunday if he carried the needed plug.

"Sure," he had replied. "Got dozens of them. But before you come in, be sure I'm there. You've never seen my shop, and you might be interested."

He knew I had been educated to be an electrical engineer. I had seen electrical repair shops before and couldn't imagine what he thought I would find especially interesting about his. They were all alike: a workbench, soldering irons, wires, heating elements, vacuum tubes, half-repaired appliances, and shelves of circuit diagram books—about as interesting as gazing at a glass of water.

I went along, however, knowing that every shop owner finds something special about his own. "I'll make sure you're there, Frank. I'd love to see your place."

This was the day I had decided to go. "I'm here to see Frank," I said to the middle-aged woman who worked the front counter.

"Can I tell him who is here?" she asked pleasantly in a typical southern drawl.

"James Chatham," I replied, "I'm here at his invitation."

"Come on back, Jim," I heard a voice from the back room. The woman ushered me through.

The scene I beheld was different from anything I would ever have expected. At a table in the middle of the room sat Frank, eating a carry-in lunch provided by the café up the street. Opposite him at the same table sat a black man about his age, eating a similar lunch. They were talking, laughing, joking, comparing notes on their work, acting as if they were both thoroughly at home in this place. A warm air of friendship flowed between them. They were obviously having a good time.

Occurrences like this absolutely did not happen in Fayette, Mississippi, in 1965. If a black man ate a meal on your property, it was "in the back" somewhere, most definitely not at the same table with you.

"This is Moses," Frank said. "I wanted you to meet him." I offered my hand to Moses. He accepted it graciously and warmly and with considerable confidence.

"Glad to meet you, Reverend," he spoke, looking me straight in the eye.

Moses was dressed in well-worn work clothes, as many others would have been on that day. But he conspicuously did not have that forlorn, beaten look that characterized other blacks. He stood erect, proud.

Frank said, "Outside these walls no one knows about Moses and me. Moses is my best friend. We've been working together for twenty-two years, and I respect him as much as any human being on earth. I sell things and he fixes them. This man is a genius. He can fix it all. You throw any problem you want at him, and he'll have it solved in a couple of hours. Don't know how he does it. All those wires and circuits are a mystery to me. He admits that television sets are a bigger challenge and that he may have trouble with some of them down the line. But so far there hasn't been anything to come through that door that Moses hasn't figured out how to fix. He's a genius!"

Moses smiled. "Frank sometimes overstates himself, Reverend," he said. "The friendship part is right, but the genius part is suspect."

Frank continued. "There's nothing in this business that Moses doesn't know about. We discuss everything. My best friend. I wanted you to meet him, because I wanted you to know that not everyone in Fayette has the same attitude."

Moses chimed in, "But we prefer, Reverend, that other people not know. It would make things hard for both Frank and me. I keep it to myself among my people, and he does the same. As far as anyone else knows, I just work here."

"Fayette will not hear it through me," I promised. I have kept that promise for more than three decades.

Two different worlds lived outside and inside that building. Outside was a caste system that told people of color that they were too inferior to be social friends with whites; inside was a rich friendship between a black man and a white man for whom color did not matter. Outside was a street full of slave descendants who drooped their heads in self-doubt; inside was one slave descendant who now held his head high in self-confidence. Outside was a dead past not yet buried; inside was a living future struggling to be born. And these two worlds, in all their enormous difference, were separated by nothing more than a twelve-inch-thick concrete-block wall. I understood fully now what Frank had wanted me to see in his electronic repair shop. I pondered the existence of such a space in downtown Fayette.

Several years later I told this story at a "convention of liberated churches" in Kansas City. A pastor from Chicago responded, "What a waste! It's too bad they never spoke out!" She wanted to know why I had not urged Frank and Moses to go public.

No, I'm sorry, it was not a waste. Here was a black man who had discovered a self he could truly be proud of, and a white man who had done the same — no small accomplishment in the human struggle. Here were two human beings who were living out what they believed in a culture that would have castigated both of them if it had found out. Here were friends who had painted a small region of beauty against a background of great ugliness. Even if they never went public, I found nothing to regret about Moses and Frank.

I am endlessly fascinated by people's private worlds, at the hidden regions we can nourish alongside what is visible. I once knew a very kind gentleman who treated his boys' Sunday school class to all sorts of expensive field trips and special events — paid for by the money he was embezzling from the store where he was the finance officer.

I knew of another man who for several years maintained one wife and family in North Carolina and another wife and family in Virginia, all of which worked very well until he decided to run for political office and the news reporters began snooping. With Frank and Moses, however, it was not evil that had to be hidden but good. That was the irony of Fayette.

Gold, Frankincense, and Myrrh

It is about 9:30 on an August evening, an hour after dark, and I am driving down a sparsely settled road outside Union Church. Cornfields on either side near their maturity, and soon the stalks will be chopped and dried for winter cattle feeding. The pavement bends sharply to the right, but I take a dirt road that continues straight ahead. Even my small Volkswagen taillights illuminate the cloud of dust behind me.

Passing through a wooded area, my headlights find the two rearview mirrors of a pickup truck parked beside a driveway. I turn into the driveway and, to my astonishment, find perhaps thirty cars and small trucks parked around the farmyard. A human figure I cannot identify, but who has already identified me, motions me to a parking place beside the farmhouse. I pull in and exit the Volkswagen. Small groups of men stand around the yard conversing in low tones. Several of them acknowledge me as I reach the front porch.

"What happened?" I inquire. The story unfolds.

Herman Galbreath, forty-eight years old, left home shortly after lunch on this Saturday to go to Brookhaven. He had told his wife, Kathrine, that he was going to the hardware store. But he must have gone other places too, because when he came driving back down that dirt road toward home at 3:45 in the afternoon, he wasn't handling the wheel any too steadily.

Amery Rutledge, the Galbreaths' next-door neighbor, came down the road behind Herman and watched him as he wavered from side to side. Suddenly, Herman stopped, and Amery stopped behind him. Amery blew his horn. In the next moment 218-pound Herman was advancing on Amery's pickup, fists clenched, eyes flaming, cursing and growling like an angry tiger. Amery, sixty-five pounds smaller, reached for his shotgun. Herman threw the cab door open and saw the gun. He clawed wildly at his neighbor just as Amery fired at point-blank range. Herman slumped to the road, dead.

No charges had been filed, and none would be, but everyone in that farmyard was wondering if Amery couldn't have figured something better to do than what he did.

I pass the yellow bug light by the front door and enter the frame house. Inside, there are women everywhere, wives of the men outside. I scan the room quickly to see if Kathrine is among them, too new in my profession to know yet that she will not be. One woman, whose face I recognize, greets me and announces my presence to the room. I am accorded general welcome.

She then leads me to the kitchen, which is laid out like an executive smorgasbord: ham, chicken, roast, turkey, corn, collards, snaps, potato salad, sliced tomatoes, home-made bread, and about twenty varieties of cakes and pies. She hands me a plate and tells me to help myself. I thank her and decline. I have been a minister only five weeks, and it will be sometime later before I discern that in this situation you eat, whether it is noon or midnight, whether you are hungry or not.

The food has been provided by the assembled gathering, the friends and neighbors of the bereaved. They have done it many times before, and they will do it many times again. Their instinct is to help in this helpless situation, so they do the one thing they know will at least help some:

bring food. They know that by tomorrow sisters and brothers and cousins and aunts and uncles will begin to gather to comfort the widow, and that all these people will have to be fed. So they set up a food line in the widow's kitchen, a sincere expression of their neighborly concern. And they stand about the house, the women inside and the men in the yard, no one saying much because there really isn't much to say, and because they don't think they are very good at saying things, anyway. But all of them saying by their presence that they know the hell this middle-aged farmer's wife is going through, because most of them have been through it themselves in one form or another, and they don't want her to have to go through it alone. They will all stay until late in the night, well after Kathrine Galbreath has gone to bed, and a few of the women will remain until relatives arrive the next day. It is a time for human solidarity, not for loneliness — the community at its best.

My hostess shows me to a bedroom where Kathrine is seated among three friends. As I enter, the three friends draw back slightly, expecting me to take the lead and believing that the widow and I should be accorded privacy if we want it. I greet them and invite the friends to stay.

"It's nice of you to come, Reverend," Kathrine says, thoughtfully conveying to me that she regards my arrival as more than just ministerial duty.

"I know this is a very hard time for you, Mrs. Galbreath," I reply. She sobs gently, acknowledging that what I have said is true.

"Would you pray with me, Reverend?" she asks. I take her hand, and then I can feel her request more clearly. "Pray with me for some light in all this cursed darkness!" she is saying. "Tell God that my head is spiraling through space and that I have no idea how to calm it down! That the life has been wrung from my body and the spirit from my soul! See if this nightmare cannot somehow be canceled, if heaven will not grant a miracle that will return the world to three o'clock this afternoon and bring Herman safely through that door! Tell God about the misery I am going through and that I doubt that I can stand it much longer!" I pray, asking for strength for Kathrine, giving thanks for the support of her family and friends.

"I was thinking just the other day," she says, "how fortunate we were. Roselynn happily married to Johnny Spencer over in Meadville, Kathrine Ann doing so well in her last year of high school, and Howard growing up to take over his father's farm someday. Everything seemed right. I was so happy. And now this. Why did it have to happen? Why did it have to happen?"

I cannot say to her, "It happened because we are all exiles from Eden, fugitives and wanderers on the earth who slay and are slain. It happened because we are all brothers and sisters of Cain, victims of the jealousy by which the first farmer killed his brother. It happened because Lamech lives within us, the spirit of vengeance against any who challenge our self-imagined importance." I cannot say these things to her, but I need not. She knows them already. She is familiar with that fundamental human instinct, so apparent in this small, quiet, Bible Belt community, to set everything straight by violence. She knows that every pickup truck in Jefferson County, Mississippi, carries a shotgun in the rear window not simply to kill buzzards. She has watched neighbor fight with neighbor before and understands that this is nothing new.

Child of the exile, mother of the crucified, wife of Auschwitz, widow of the war dead—your voice is one and its sound is everywhere. Your question joins the pleas of people in all ages who have walked the valley of the shadow of a loved one's violent death and cried out, "When, O God, can the killing stop? When will the creation be reborn? When will that wretched horror that seizes and twists the heart stalk us no longer?"

In answer, God's promise is spoken. God spoke it a long time ago—to Abraham and Sarah, to Peter and Paul—and it has been around all this time. But it is heard most vividly when the heart is tuned, by those who can go no further without it, because without this promise there is no reason to go further. Kathrine Galbreath is at this place right now.

> They shall beat their swords into plowshares,
>   and their spears into pruning hooks;
> Nation shall not lift up weapon against nation,
>   nor learn violence anymore.
> But men and women shall rest under their vines
>   and under their fig trees;
> Farmers shall harvest what they plant,
>   and families shall enjoy the cool fall breezes,
>   sitting in thatch-back rocking chairs on their porches,
>   watching the grandchildren play in the front yard,
> And none shall make them afraid;
>   violence shall disrupt them no more.
> The mouth of the Lord has said this!

The empty vision of an idealist? Perhaps. Maybe we are foolish to record such poetry in holy writ and teach it to our children. But consider: are there not signs, hidden but unmistakable, of its coming? Look, for instance, at the assembled group standing around this farmyard right now. And look at the gifts they have brought: gold, frankincense, and myrrh, presented to one who now loses her life as a sign that she will regain it. Their act is God's promise. Their instinct for human relatedness is God's building stone. Their sturdiness is God's power. Their graciousness is God's love. These Mississippi farm people, best known across the nation in this tumultuous year of 1964 as southern rednecks—their presence is God's promise, to you, Kathrine Galbreath, a veiled but sure sign of what is to come.

> He shall feed his flock like a shepherd,
>   and gather the lambs in his arms,
> And carry them in his bosom,
>   and gently feed those that are with young.
>
> Isaiah 40:11

This is the word that the Lord has spoken, and the ambassadors of the Lord silently proclaim that word to all with ears to hear.

Cry the bitter cries of grief, Kathrine Galbreath! Lament your loss and struggle with your difficult future. But know that God will come and wipe away every tear from your eyes and that mourning and crying and pain and death shall be no more. Yes, the mouth of the Lord has spoken it!

We talk briefly of funeral arrangements. I greet Howard Galbreath, strapping fifteen-year-old who appears from the back of the house to be with his mother. Kathrine thanks me again for coming. And I leave, very sad at the grief, but also a tiny bit joyful at the sheer beauty of what I have seen.

Each in Its Time

Miss Lottie, of Union Church, was a case study in human devotion. She and her older sister, Miss Lucy, had spent their adult lives living together in the same five-room frame house. Miss Lucy had been a schoolteacher, bringing home cash income. Miss Lottie had done all the domestic things—shopping, cooking, cleaning, yard work, and gardening. Gregarious, gracious, energetic women, they were both much beloved in the Union Church community.

At age seventy-one, Miss Lucy, who was slowly becoming blind, had an accident that paralyzed her legs. It was a wrenching turning point in their lives; everything would be different afterward. Without question or hesitation, however, Miss Lottie had converted her older sister's bedroom to provide for her future care. They would continue to live together just as they had in the past; there was no thought of any other arrangement.

Miss Lottie, slight of stature but a seemingly endless well of strength and stamina, had thrown herself into caring for her sister as if it were her life calling. Miss Lottie cooked and served the meals, knowing exactly what Miss Lucy liked and how she liked it. Miss Lottie kept the sheets cleaned and the bedclothes changed. She administered the medicine. She read to her sister, talked to her, and selected radio music for her to listen to, stimulating her mind to keep the engine tuned. She was the hostess for the unending procession of friends who dropped by to visit. Never—literally never—did Lottie leave Lucy for more than a couple of hours to go to lunch at a neighbor's house or to worship in church, and then some trusted friend would handle the watch.

I marveled at Miss Lottie's devotion. She seemed completely content with her role in life, approaching every task every day with good humor and pleasantness. With all the people I knew who spent their lives complaining, here was one woman who had plenty of reason to complain but never did. Self-pity was not in her vocabulary.

Lottie expressed great interest in the people who came to visit her. In talking to me, for example, she would inquire about my work, my family, my experiences, my opinions. I had, several years before, spent a summer working as an electrical engineer on Cape Cod, and Miss Lottie wanted to learn all I could tell her about the cape's landscape. She had a very intense way of communicating her interest by looking straight into your eyes and listening to every word.

A more devoted and gracious woman I have never met. Union Church — humble southern village that it was — had raised her well in the best of the human graces.

One day Miss Lucy died, of no particular cause. She just quietly eased off into eternity.

We held the community visitation and the funeral at their home. Union Church poured out to show its love and respect for these two sisters who were so much a part of the village family. Lottie mourned Lucy's loss and accepted with great appreciation the empathy of their friends. Flowers came from all directions; food was everywhere. The procession to the cemetery was the largest in anyone's memory. It was a totally fitting occasion for the passage of a favorite daughter.

I wondered as I watched if this would be Miss Lottie's final performance, if she — tough little woman though she was — would not quietly slide downhill now that her daily raison d'ĕtre had been taken away. Would she find herself without motivation and discreetly decide to join her sister? I had seen it happen to others. I resolved to come back in a few days to check on her.

On my next visit to Union Church, I knocked at her door. I almost did not recognize the woman who answered. It was Miss Lottie, completely dolled up in a tweed suit, new shoes, and a very stylish fur hat. She looked stunning. She was tugging a loaded suitcase across the living room floor toward the front door. "Oh, Reverend," she exclaimed. "I'm glad you came, but I'll have to ask you to come back when I return home. I have signed up for a train trip across the Canadian Rockies, and James McBee is picking me up to take me to the Jackson airport. I thought you were James. Would you mind moving this suitcase over by the front door? And would you promise to come back in three weeks after I get home? I've wanted to see the Canadian Rockies all my life, and I'll tell you all about them. Although, when I get home, I won't be here long. After a little bit I'm going to visit my cousin's daughter in Toronto. She's been wanting me to come for a long time, and I'm going to do it. I'll be back in about two months. Can you come see me then? Yes, please set the suitcase there by the door. James will get it."

Lottie was not about to sit at home and rust, obsessing on which medicines the doctor had prescribed on her last visit. She was ready for the world, and now it was time! No worry that her 102-pound frame might be blown away by a Chicago wind. No worry that she would have to squint to see the Rockies. Lottie was off! The way she had transformed herself, she might even find a pleasant gentleman to sit next to on the train and strike up a conversation! Even at eighty-six, it's all in how you think about yourself!

"Sure, Miss Lottie, I said, "I'll come back in two months." Why had I ever worried?

From Miss Susie's Front Porch

Miss Susie Grafton of Union Church was an eighty-seven-year-old farm woman with a keen mind and a prodigious spirit. I wish she had lived seventy years later, as her imagination would have thrived and exhilarated in the new era of opportunity among women. Perhaps a piece of her still does live. Her great-niece and namesake, Sue Grafton, is a nationally acclaimed writer of murder mysteries, and I like to think that some of Miss Susie's style is still expressing itself.

Miss Susie had lived her entire adult life alone in a very simple house on the main road leading into Union Church from Fayette. In 1964 her house could definitely have used a new paint job, although the siding was of wood tough enough that it probably would have lasted another twenty or thirty years. Her property was typical: an acre of land, grown up around the edges, the remnants of an old barn still visible in back and a long unused outhouse decaying in the far corner. Her front porch spanned the full length of the house and held four rocking chairs where she visited with friends.

From that porch, Miss Susie had watched seventy-five years of the community's life come and go. She knew everyone and everything. She was a quiet, graceful woman, devoutly religious and respectful of all persons around her, but once you got her talking, you were in for a fascinating afternoon. She was held in fond regard by her entire community.

Miss Susie's father, Dr. C. W. Grafton, had been pastor of the Union Church Presbyterian Church for sixty-two years. He had never served a moment anywhere else. From that ninety-member congregation, Dr. Grafton had risen to high prominence in his denomination, elected in the early 1900s as moderator of the Presbyterian General Assembly.

Dr. Grafton had died in 1935, but in Union Church you couldn't tell it. His spirit still moved powerfully over the village, fashioning its thinking and its way of life. I used to hear an unending litany, Dr. Grafton said this, Dr. Grafton thought that, Dr. Grafton believed so-and-so. Even with Dr. Grafton so long gone, many still would not have dared transgress his wishes.

Dr. Grafton's Scottish ethics seem to have centered on two matters: Sabbath and sex. Any transgression of the Sabbath, of any sort or degree, would call down the fire of heaven. No one was to do even a mite of work on Sunday, and no one was to cause anyone else to work: "thou, nor thy son, nor thy daughter, nor thy manservant, nor thy maidservant, nor thy ox, nor thy donkey, nor the stranger that is within thy gate."

There were at least two Union Church families that still strictly honored this tradition. Almost every Sunday, my wife, Nancy, and I would be invited to someone's home for dinner after morning worship. On one particular Sunday we arrived at a family's house to find that the entire dinner — country ham, chicken and dumplings, green beans, corn, okra, squash, corn bread, and pies — had been prepared on Saturday and laid out on the dining room table overnight. We were to sit down and eat it just as it sat, no warming, no carrying it from the kitchen, no salting, no peppering, no nothing except for lifting off the light paper napkins that had tried to protect it from the flies. It was, to say the least, a strange meal, but our hosts saw nothing strange in it at all. When we finished, we replaced the napkin coverings, got up from the table, and adjourned to the living room. The food and dishes were left until Monday.

This happened in two different households we visited. Nancy and I wondered each time if Sunday prayers in Union Church were effective against food poisoning.

Sex, in Dr. Grafton's ethics, was to be treated even more severely than the Sabbath. Sexual activity, though necessary for procreation, was innately evil. You lived a much more righteous and pure life if you avoided it totally. If, as Paul the Apostle said, you absolutely had to get married, then you should do so, to prevent sin. (Dr. Grafton had.) But it was far better to abstain if possible. Sex, it was believed, took a person's mind and heart away from devotion to the Lord and caused preoccupation with the flesh rather than the spirit. Merely looking on a woman lustfully was sin; the Lord himself had said so. You could keep your heart more pure, more focused on God, more safe for eternal reward, if you stayed completely away from sex's allure.

The result of this belief, and easily the most distinguishing feature of the Union Church community, was the number of old, never-married people who lived there. The McArn family consisted of five single brothers and sisters, all between ages seventy-five and ninety, who had spent their lives living unmarried in one house. One sister, Mrs. McKell, had married early but had moved back with her siblings after her husband died. Miss Lottie and Miss Lucy Warren had never married. Mr. Jack Thompson, Miss Cecilia Evans, Miss Susie Grafton herself, and numerous others were lifelong singles. The effect, of course, was that for half a century, the period of Dr. Grafton's leadership, the community had been dying out. As with the Shakers in Kentucky, the final outcome of all this purity would be self-inflicted termination.

Dr. Grafton's daughter, Miss Susie, was a storehouse of information on the past. More than a few afternoons I sat in one of her front porch rocking chairs coaxing the memories out of her. It was one of my most pleasant duties.

"Did I tell you," she related one day, "about the visiting preacher who got himself in real, deep trouble? He had preached at church in the morning. But it was a real hot day, so he had changed his shirt to go visiting in the afternoon. His second shirt had a tiny tint of blue in it, not much but enough to see. I remember it well; I thought it was pretty. The McKenzies, the grandparents of the people who live up the road now, thought it was positive sacrilege, that this man was trying to be ostentatious and show off, that he had no respect for being a servant of the Lord. They chastised him on the spot for bringing this disgrace against God into their house, and then they called for the whole church to consider the matter. There was a big meeting. Some people thought it was serious and others didn't. But that visiting preacher wasn't ever invited back. And the next time one was, the elders made sure he didn't bring any blue shirts with him. It was the biggest scandal in Union Church that whole decade."

"You may have noticed," Miss Susie recounted on another occasion, "that among the older members of our church the women still sit on the right-hand side and men sit on the left in Sunday worship. The younger ones don't do it any longer — their families all sit together — but the older ones still do. It comes from the belief that you need to keep your mind clear and pure during worship. My father felt that way strongly. If you mix men and women, they start thinking about one another, catching a peek here and a glance there and pondering other things than what they should be thinking about. They don't pay attention to the sermon, and they let their minds wander off during the prayers — no real devotion to God. True worship requires single-mindedness; 'You cannot worship God and mammon.' So we split right and left as soon as we walk in the back door of the church.

My generation got so used to it that now we wouldn't feel right doing anything else."

Miss Susie continued. "Reverend, we Scotch Presbyterians have always suspected deep down that sex is wrong, certainly outside marriage, but probably also inside marriage. It comes from one text in the Bible: 'I was born in iniquity, and in sin did my mother conceive me' [Psalm 51:5]. David wrote that, and it's the clearest statement you can find. If David's conception came by sin, despite the fact that his parents were married, then there is no other interpretation you can give it. Sex has to be evil. The virgin birth was the final proof. God didn't want his son born by sin, so he arranged for it to happen without any sex. The only pure and spotless one ever created came into this world in a pure and spotless way. For years this community believed that to the bottom of our hearts, but now with the younger ones it doesn't seem to matter very much. I think they have a different way of looking at things. Sometimes I think some of them would be better off if they still looked at it our way."

Miss Susie's stories ranged over many subjects. "Do you know, Reverend, about the communists who are getting ready to take over Union Church? There's a group of ladies down Perth Road who don't have anything better to do than listen to that Dr. Carl who preaches on the radio every morning. He comes out of New Jersey, and he's got these women stirred up over how thoroughly the communists have infiltrated the government. They're going to use the Internal Revenue Service to charge us about twenty times as much tax as we actually owe so they can seize our farms and walk away with everything. Dr. Carl laid the whole story out clear as crystal on his radio show

85

last week. Said we should expect these people to be coming after us pretty soon now. Said if we want to fight it, we should send him as much money as we can, because he knows all about it, and he will do the fighting for us.

"These women have been sending their money to that Dr. Carl for years. They get a retirement check and send half of it to this man on the radio who doesn't know them at all. Ella Mae Buford, I'll swear, if she's sent a dime, she's sent fifty thousand dollars. She mailed two hundred last week to help Dr. Carl launch helium balloons across Russia with Bible verses tied to them. Martha Jean in the post office told me that Ella Mae sends a check every Tuesday morning.

"I think Dr. Carl ought to be ashamed of himself scaring these poor old ladies half to death to get their money. And they're nice women, too, nothing wrong with them. Been friends of mine all their lives. Their only mistake is believing what that fancy-tongued radio preacher tells them."

Miss Susie knew all the latest. "Last night Miss Edna up the road almost had a conniption fit. She's losing her faculties a little bit anyway. But she woke up in the middle of the night, sat straight up in bed, and started yelling, 'The darkies are coming! The darkies are coming!' A noise outside the house had awakened her, and that was her first reaction. She sat there about five minutes in a kind of daze, and then suddenly her eyes popped wide open, and it all happened again, only this time with even more alarm in her voice, 'The darkies are coming!'

"You see, Reverend, white folks all over the South have long suspected deep in our hearts that someday the black people are all going to band together and come after us, to rape us and kill us. It'll be retaliation for what's happened to them. People don't talk about it much, but it's a deep fear we learned when we were young. It was a leftover from the Civil War, only back then it was the Yankees that were coming with the darkies behind them. That noise in her sleep brought that old memory straight out of Miss Edna."

Miss Susie's memory went on. "We had a crisis during World War II at the church. Mighty few men left to serve as elders on the Session [the church's governing board] — a handful of real old ones, but they were dying out fast. The Session got down to three men at one time, and we didn't know what we were going to do."

"Any chance you could have elected a woman?" I asked.

"Oh, naw! We'd never do that. The Bible says it's got to be a man. There's no self-respecting woman in this community who would even consider taking the job when it's against God's will. Don't worry. No matter how desperate we get, we'll always find us a man somewhere!"

"Reverend, I attended the most unusual funeral several years ago—I guess it was about twenty years ago. Something happened that I've never forgotten. This old black farmer named Elijah had died over near Meadville. He didn't have much, but he did have his wife, Rosie, who used to work for me. That's why I went, because I loved Rosie dearly. She was up in her seventies by the time Elijah passed.

"Anyway, it was a pretty usual funeral. It was held in Rosie's church, and that place was packed with their relatives and friends. After the preacher finished, we all walked out to the graveyard and put Elijah in the ground. Then everyone just stood around and talked for a long time, trying to comfort poor Rosie—she was in great grief—and trying to assure her that things would be okay for her.

"Then the most remarkable thing happened. This car came up the road and parked. A man got out and came walking toward Rosie. She was sitting in a chair by the grave. When he got to where she was, he bent down on one knee and started talking to her. 'Miss Rosie, I know that you miss your husband dreadfully and that his loss is going to be the hardest thing you have ever had to endure. I'm deeply sorry for the pain you are going through, and I want to extend my deepest sympathy in your time of bereavement.

" 'I do want you to know, however, that your husband was a very caring and loving man. There was nothing he wanted in his life more than that his dear wife should be well taken care of after he was gone. I am, therefore, here today to deliver to you what he provided.

" 'Elijah bought a life insurance policy and named you as the beneficiary, Miss Rosie.'

"At that point the man started counting one-dollar bills into Rosie's lap. 'One, two, three . . . '

"The people around were a little stunned, waiting to see what would happen.

" '. . . ten, eleven, twelve . . .'

"The collected gathering began to realize that this man was serious.

" '. . . eighteen, nineteen, twenty, twenty-one . . .'

"The eyes got bigger.

" '. . . forty-five, forty-six, forty-seven, forty-eight . . .'

"How long was this going to keep up?

" '. . . 106, 107, 108 . . .'

"The dollar bills were falling off both sides of Rosie's lap, and they had to get a paper bag to help her hold them.

" '. . . 215, 216, 217 . . .'

This was more money than poor old Rosie had ever seen in her life.

"'...346, 347, 348...'

"The whole place by now was dancing with joy for Rosie. They had thought she would have to scrape together her next meal.

"When that man reached five hundred, he stopped. Then he said, 'Miss Rosie, I know that money cannot take the place of your dear Elijah. He was the man of your heart, and no amount of this world's possessions can ever take the place of him. But because of his care for you, you do not have to worry about worldly goods. Your heart can rest in peace knowing that you have been cared for by your faithful husband.'

"With that, the man quietly departed.

He wasn't even able to make it to his car. People crowded up to him, wanting his insurance. He must have signed up twenty more policies before he left that day. I'm sure that man never spent a dollar on advertising!"

Miss Susie always returned to Papa, just as the entire community did. "My Papa was a kind man; I always loved him. But he was rigid in his ideas of right and wrong. He used to preach once a month out at Perth—there was a little Presbyterian chapel out there. On Saturday afternoon he would mount his horse, ride out, stay over Saturday night with someone, and preach on Sunday. Then he would wait until Monday morning, do some visiting around Perth, and ride back here to Union Church late Monday afternoon. We missed him dreadfully while he was gone, especially if it was the cold of winter and things needed to be tended to.

"The best day of my Papa's life was the day Mr. Ford's automobile finally came to Union Church. Papa bought one, and it changed his life. The Bible specifically forbade a person from making his horse work on Sunday, but it didn't say anything against making his automobile work. Papa could drive that car all he wanted. Now he went out to Perth early Sunday morning, preached, visited, and came home Sunday night. It was a lot better for all of us."

Thus Did the Lord Say

John was a Union Church farmer, not a modern farmer with seeders and reapers and an airplane to spread insecticide, but an old-time farmer who broke up clods with a mule and picked corn ears one by one. A harder-working man never lived. John had built his own house at a cost of six hundred dollars. You could tell it somewhat by looking at it; the walls leaned slightly and the ventilation increased some every year. But seldom did it occur to a south Mississippi farmer that the temperature inside needed to be drastically different from the temperature outside.

Whenever I went to see John, I would always find him working in the field. He knew that his life and welfare depended on that ground, and he did his best to take care of it.

John's greatest difficulty, however, was that he was acutely high strung. He worried about absolutely everything: whether the worms would destroy this year's bean plants, whether the drought would turn his field into a hardened brick, whether the Washington bureaucrats would try to seize his farm to pay off the national debt, whether the communists were about to send missiles and nuclear bombs over the horizon at him, whether Seth, the third son of Adam and Eve, had populated the world by incest, and whether any of his corn was being used to make bootleg mash, which he was sure would result in the Lord striking him dead.

You might as well let John be the Sunday school teacher, because he was going to do most of the talking anyway. You could count on about ten minutes of anti-communist tirade, but beyond that it became a pretty good experience. John always had some story to tell that might or might not have anything to do with the week's Bible passage.

After considerable coaxing, a couple of John's friends persuaded him one day to see a psychiatrist in Jackson. He had been more high strung than usual lately, and his friends were worried that it would affect his health. John placed no trust in the medical profession, especially in psychiatrists. He wasn't even sure he knew what they were: "Get paid all that money for just listening?" But he finally consented to go. He came back reporting that the psychiatrist had told him that he had a severe case of "annexity."

One day John began to worry about whether he would ever find a wife. He had been looking for one for a long time without any success. He had prayed as hard as he could that the Lord would lead him to the right one. He knew it would be terrible and wrong to be married to anyone other than the Lord's pick. He approached the whole matter with great concern.

The next time he was in Brookhaven doing his shopping, the Lord stopped John dead in his tracks and said to him, "John, do you see that woman standing over there by the five-and-dime store? She is the woman I want you to marry. You'll have to figure out how to make your approach, but she is definitely the one."

John walked up to the woman and said, "Pardon me, Mam, but the Lord just told me I'm supposed to marry you." It was, everyone agreed, an unorthodox approach, but it apparently worked. John and Hallie were married a few weeks later.

Hallie was as sturdy as John was erratic. Whenever he got riled up, she got calmed down. He would go into one of his anticommunist tirades at the dinner table, and she would quietly ask if anyone wanted tea and haul him off to the kitchen to crack ice. He would want to march off to battle against Bobby Kennedy, and she would shuttle him away to change the baby's diaper. He worried and she trusted. He doubted and she believed. She was the rock that anchored their small farm through the unending earthquakes of John's nervousness.

After twenty years they had three fine children, a namesake son who worked the fields as hard as his father and two daughters who were as responsible and kind as a couple of farm young people could ever be. John's health was good, the fields still bore their produce, and Hallie, tall and regal, reigned as the guiding spirit over the entire proceeding, still sorting out for John what mattered from all that didn't.

It was nearly a miracle, that "severe annexity" could produce such a splendid result. The only possible conclusion was that John had been right, that God really had told him to marry Hallie on that day in Hattiesburg, and that any of us who were skeptical had had too much theological education. I have forever since been more careful of what I snicker at.

The Scots' Legacy

From my first visit to Union Church, I heard about Dr. Stevens. Dr. Stevens was a retired physician, at that time in his late eighties. He had served the Union Church community through his whole career. He had delivered all the babies, tended all the deaths, and treated all the illnesses. He didn't care much for hospitals. There was one in Brookhaven, but he considered it a measure of last resort. In his mind sick people belonged at home, around their kin, where things were familiar. His main medicine was relationship, although not warmth. It was hierarchical relationship, and he was definitely at the top of the hierarchy. With Dr. Grafton gone, his younger friend, Dr. Stevens, had taken over as the community's leading authority—not just on medicine but on everything from politics to theology.

The occasion on which I visited the Union Church Presbyterian Church to preach a trial sermon had to be set at a time when Dr. Stevens could be there; otherwise, no one would be sure how to vote. I remember that first sermon well. It was February, and the worship was held in the church annex because the main sanctuary building had no heat. It was Sunday evening and getting cold. The potbellied stove was doing its best, but the building had not been designed for heat efficiency. About thirty chairs were assembled in a semicircle around the makeshift pulpit from which I was to preach. As people arrived—I was clearly the prime show in the village that night—the atmosphere warmed. They were in a mood to be nice, and I, a tobacco farmer's grandson, knew innately how to be nice in return.

Having heard all day about Dr. Stevens, I kept scanning the gathering to try to identify him. I should have known better. Back in high school our basketball coach had said, "The best way to be significant is to be late. If you arrive early, the sense of anticipation never has the opportunity to build." Dr. Stevens had learned that lesson long ago. He would arrive when he would arrive, and the proceeding would not start until he did.

Finally the moment came. The annex door swung open, and the entrance was nearly regal. He, accompanied by Mrs. Stevens and aided by a friend, hobbled in slowly, using a cane but with his shining silver hair and his innate air of authority leaving no doubt. He greeted his friends cordially. They stood aside to let him choose where he wanted to sit. He sat dead in the middle in the second row, right in front of my eyes. There was no doubt who the jury was.

I preached, nervously. Apparently I passed. Dr. Stevens smiled and greeted me warmly when it was over and told me he thought I had done a fine job. I was appreciative and relieved. Seminary had been nothing like this.

Dr. Stevens would show up in church only rarely after that. My trial sermon had been virtually his final public appearance. But the aura of authority persisted all over the village.

Several of the families in Union Church bore a remarkably distinct characteristic, and Dr. Stevens's family was a perfect example. One generation would be highly disciplined, highly accomplished, highly regarded, and the next generation would be drowned in tragedy, usually involving alcohol.

My doorbell rang one day, and the man standing there introduced himself as Howard Stevens. I had never met him before. Howard said he had not lived in Union Church for years, but now he had come home. Instead of medicine, like his father, he had chosen music, his great love. He had earned a master's degree and then a Ph.D. at Louisiana State University. He had performed and taught music quite successfully. He had written and published a number of musical scores.

But running through it all had been his alcoholism. He had left home for college with a very strong sense of how much his father expected of him and of how much he needed to succeed—especially since he was pursuing a field that seemed "soft" to his father. Howard had worked hard, pushing himself relentlessly. He had succeeded quite well, becoming known in his field. But he could never quite please his father. Music was the wrong thing; no matter how good he became, his father would not understand.

He had started drinking during his junior year at LSU, mostly to calm his anxiety. It became the one way he could calm down. Had he ever drunk at home, his father would have killed him. He had kept it carefully hidden.

Howard had married, and his wife had borne three children. His drinking had come more under control during that time. Life seemed good, and he was less anxious. But then the anxiety had resurfaced. And so had the alcoholism.

After several years, his wife had announced that she had had all she was going to take. She demanded that he move out. He had done so, still keeping his career, however, fairly well in tact. That situation had worked for a while, but it finally fell apart. He had been fired from his teaching position.

For the past few years, Howard had been living off temporary work, playing with this music group or that, teaching a seminar when he could get asked to do so, taking on a private student here or there, piecing life together one day at a time. Through all of this, he had kept up the pretense before his father that everything was fine, that he was simply too busy to visit very often. It was a pathetic pretense—he knew and felt that deeply.

·

And then the bomb had dropped. In a routine physical examination, Howard had been diagnosed as having a huge, cancerous growth in his lung. He had also been a chronic smoker, and he had feared cancer for years. He was terrified. He knew he was dying; there was nothing medicine could do for him. He also knew that he had made a monumental mess of his life. He had come back home, to where it all began, to see if he could set right what had gone dreadfully wrong. He had hoped to find his father a less exacting, more understanding, more approving person. But, no, just the opposite was the case. As with many of us, advancing years had only made Dr. Stevens more the way he had always been. Howard had found no absolution.

It was true tragedy. Dr. Stevens had both created and destroyed his son with the same Scottish rigor. Howard both loved and hated his father for the same reasons.

Howard and I charted out some things he could do in his final time to feel better about himself. The main thing was for him to give free piano lessons to every child in Union Church who wanted them. He could at least make some gift back to the community. He taught those lessons to four children on the old upright piano in the annex of Union Church Presbyterian Church, on an instrument far beneath his talents. It was the same building where, fourteen months earlier, his father had subjected me to thorough examination.

Howard died quietly in the Veterans Administration hospital in Jackson, essentially — and perhaps mercifully — out of his mind by the time it happened.

His children did not come to their father's funeral. I never met them. I have not tracked their paths and have no idea what has happened to them. But I suspect I know. They reacted strongly against their father's alcoholism, vowing that they themselves would never fall victim to such degradation. Through hard work and devotion, they became rigorous, accomplished people, achieving in life and thinking that similar success should be within everyone's reach. And then they raised the generation of their own children. And these children chafed under the high, self-righteous expectations of their parents and were unable to live up to them. And Howard was reborn.

That's the way it seemed to happen in Union Church. It was the blessing and the curse of the Scots; the community could not escape either one.

Nighttime Radio

Except for Little League baseball games in the summer, Fayette shut down at five o'clock in the afternoon. All the stores, the offices, the two restaurants, the gas stations, the laundry, the public library—everyone went home. There was one place open until 11:00 P.M. out on the highway about two miles north of town, Brown's One Stop, where you could buy an ice cream sandwich and sit in the parking lot and eat it. But that was the only thing open for miles.

Therefore, a lot of people listened to nighttime radio. Jackson, eighty-five miles away, still had only two television stations, and we were on the fringe of their coverage area.

Nighttime radio had several offerings. There were the St. Louis Hawks basketball games on station KMOX—it was the glory days of 6' 10" miracle man Bob Pettit, and every male teenager in Fayette, white and black, nurtured the dream of playing for the Hawks, which none of them ever did.

Nighttime radio also offered Reverend Ike out of WWVA in Wheeling, West Virginia. Reverend Ike was there to convince you that God wanted you to be successful, just as God had made Reverend Ike successful. He would describe all the wonderful things he owned, from his Cadillac to his vacation cottage in the Virgin Islands, and how much he enjoyed them. And if you would send Reverend Ike enough money, to make him even more successful, Reverend Ike would show you how to do it for yourself, how to have a positive self-image and positive expectations for yourself. That was the key.

Nighttime radio broadcast Brother and Sister Ivy out of Shreveport, Louisiana. Brother and Sister would take any personal problem you might have and tell you the Lord's will for it. Any dilemma, any question: Brother and Sister had searched the Bible over on every possible subject, and they could deliver the final word. And they would gladly do it for a small contribution to support their humble ministry. Brother and Sister Ivy treated everyone like six-year-olds, talking in a completely overstated, melodic tone that overemphasized every word. But they seemed to get away with it. They were on for a full hour every night, and they must have spent the rest of the day counting their contributions.

And, finally, nighttime radio offered Eddie Roy Pegram, God's evangelist to twentieth-century America, out of some station in Oklahoma. Eddie Roy could flat lay it on. He was convinced that America was living in mortal sin and that the days of God's retribution were at hand. He could pick any subject—adultery, cheating, strong drink, smoking, greed—and prophesy like Jeremiah.

Whatever it was, the nation was guilty of it, and Eddie Roy had the power to shine God's light of righteousness into its darkest corners. He was relentless. You didn't turn him on unless your ears were ready for an old-fashioned blistering.

After we moved to Winston-Salem several years later, a local Bible college held a revival in the Reynolds High School auditorium, the largest auditorium in town. The Bible college enrolled probably two hundred students, and they had decided they wanted to demonstrate to their student body what real preaching was like. They invited Eddie Roy Pegram to be the guest evangelist.

Because we had heard him on the radio in Fayette, Nancy and I decided to go. We sat off in a wing of the auditorium where we could leave if it turned out to be boring. It wasn't!

Eddie Roy preached that night on the evils of sex education in the public schools. He drew lurid word pictures of the things America's children were being taught, of the photographs in their textbooks and the permissive, promiscuous ideas being set forth to them by our teachers. His descriptions were like something out of *Playboy* magazine. He gave graphic detail on every evil he had uncovered in his investigations. And to think, our tax dollars were supporting this filth, our politicians were voting for it, our school boards were adopting it, our teachers were teaching it—and, worst of all, our innocent, impressionable children were being ruined by it. A whole generation of young ones was being taught that sex was perfectly okay with anyone they wanted, anytime they wanted, anywhere they wanted, for any reason they wanted. "That's what our public schools are teaching!" Eddie Roy roared to the overflowing approval of his listeners. "It'll be the ruin of this country! The brimstone of God almighty will rain down upon us in holy retribution for this grossest of all abominations!"

Through the entire ninety-minute sermon, the front twenty rows of faculty and students sat at rapt attention, tongues nearly hanging out, breath quickened, eyes fixed, minds glued on the subject matter. It was a kind of sustained, mass orgy, with everyone's imagination running wild. Eddie Roy had showed them how to preach, all right — at least how to weave compelling word pictures. There was a great sense of release when it was over. The entire auditorium erupted in celebration that this magnificent servant of the Lord was able to deliver the gospel so eloquently. The country might well be saved if a few more like him could be raised to the Lord's service!

We heard nothing more of Eddie Roy for several years after that. We didn't travel in those circles, and he did not come in on our car radio in North Carolina.

Then one day we saw an article about him in a national news magazine. Eddie Roy had decided to create his own Bible university in the Southwest. He had appealed to his radio listeners for support, and they had responded generously, coming forward with several million dollars. The first buildings had been built, and the university was now in its fourth year. Its first graduating class had received its diplomas only weeks before.

And a particularly touching graduation it had been. The two top students, the best Eddie Roy had produced, had graduated in the morning and married each other that afternoon. Valedictory diplomas at 11:00, marriage vows at 4:00, with, of course, Eddie Roy Pegram presiding at both. The entire community had been charmed.

But then the unexpected had happened. Before the newlyweds had joined in their marriage bed that evening, they had decided they should cleanse themselves, before God and before each other. They had agreed to confess the worst sins they had ever committed, the darkest blotches on their records, so that neither one would ever be surprised. Thus, they would launch this new relationship in the right direction.

To their mutual amazement, they both confessed the same thing: the worst thing each had ever done was spend the night making love with Eddie Roy Pegram.

That ended the marriage and the university. I never heard Eddie Roy Pegram on the radio again.

Winston-Salem, North Carolina

1966–1973

Interstate 85 is the major north-south thoroughfare running from Petersburg, Virginia, through Durham, Greensboro, and Charlotte, North Carolina, and Atlanta, Georgia. Winston-Salem is about twenty-five miles off this main route. That was Winston-Salem's major character: it was always about twenty-five miles off the main route.

Centered on the headquarters of the R. J. Reynolds Tobacco Company, Winston-Salem simply moved slower than other towns. The Reynolds family still lived in the city and took a strong and direct hand in what happened there. Winston-Salem, as a result, was attractive, green, a bit cultured, graceful, settled, hierarchical, and extremely patronizing. People called it a very pretty place, but no one ever characterized it as a wellspring of opportunity for newly emerging ideas.

We moved to Winston-Salem as hope and idealism were sweeping the country. Recently passed civil rights laws provided new opportunity for black America. The women's rights movement was close behind. President Lyndon Johnson's war on poverty was building low-income housing and new neighborhoods across the country. Job-training programs were being established. Federal money was pouring into antipoverty work. The president's "Great Society," following President John F. Kennedy's "New Frontier," provided a vision we all wanted to believe in.

"Yes, we can really make a difference!" young people believed. The youth of this nation turned out in unprecedented numbers: to walk in demonstrations, to build and repair houses, to join the Peace Corps, to work for voter registration, to tutor poor children. The nation's leadership articulated a strong devotion to raising the less fortunate out of poverty. Young people stepped forward to commit, believing that their personal efforts could build a better America.

Rarely do moments like this occur, when genuine optimism floods into our collective heart and the individual feels worthwhile. Most often cynicism and self-centeredness rule. But in the 1960s the youth of this nation *believed*. It was an exciting time.

Clouding the horizon, however, was Vietnam. Very shortly, these same 1960s young people would decide that we had no business in that tiny, faraway Southeast Asian country. "Defending the freedom of freedom-loving people," spraying napalm, and "destroying villages to save them" were not causes they wished to die for. Many draftees would refuse to go, choosing prison or Canada instead. The heart of the nation would deeply divide over the Vietnam War.

My Winston-Salem job was to bring affluent people and poor people together, to devise ways that suburban Presbyterians could make helpful contributions to the antipoverty effort and that poor people could help educate suburbanites. I worked with a twenty-five-member house church in the affluent end of town and in a residential neighborhood called Eleventh Street Bottom in the low-income end of town. I worked beside a young colleague named Jimmie who had grown up in the Bottom. I constantly saw both sides of life.

Eleventh Street Bottom had been constructed in the early 1900s as a real estate investment by several wealthy families. Into it and similar neighborhoods had poured hundreds of black laborers recruited by Reynolds Tobacco from the cotton fields of South Carolina and Georgia. The Bottom consisted of street after street of very modest frame houses, many of them three-room duplexes. The original builders of the neighborhood had kept their properties in reasonable repair. Following generations had not done so well. Eleventh Street Bottom had become a classic slum. More than 80 percent of the property was owned by absentee slumlords, and most of it was maintained very poorly.

The Bottom consisted of two hillsides that joined in the middle. The average family income was the lowest in the city. It was a run-down, sorry place to live. But about three thousand families called it home.

It took a lot of strength, a lot of savvy, to survive in the Bottom. Most of the city thought of the people who lived there as ignorant. They were not particularly well educated formally, but they were most assuredly not ignorant. They had carefully honed skills and great expertise at surviving within their environment, an environment in which I don't think I could have survived for long. The Bottom's citywide reputation — as the roughest neighborhood in town — resulted mostly from myths blown vastly out of proportion.

I found the Bottom to be populated by genuine folks who were trying their best to make their way through life. A few continued to work for Reynolds Tobacco, a few more for downtown businesses, others were retired, and others yet drew welfare.

I worked the streets of Eleventh Street Bottom day and night for seven years and never once had any violence threatened against me or my automobile. This time was before the proliferation drugs and guns.

Religious denominations in the mid-1960s were feeling deep guilt pangs about having done virtually nothing about either race relations or poverty despite the religious prosperity of the 1950s. Churches were establishing many kinds of experimental ministries in a tardy but sincere effort to see what they could do. Mine was one.

The twenty-five people in my house church tended to be well educated, innovative people — not possessing the laissez faire attitude prevalent in most of white Winston-Salem. Many were escaping churches they had found self-centered and dull and were searching for a more vital mode. We were suspect across the city: a church that worshiped on Thursday night, possessed no property, did not appear in the telephone book, and was more concerned with what happened in this life than in the hereafter. It did not compute. In many quarters, it still doesn't.

Winston-Salem, most of all, cued me to the importance of basics. Do people have food? Do they have clothes? Do they have homes? Do they have some money? Do their children have a future? Much of prosperous America forgets how important these questions are, preoccupied as we are with which dress we will wear, which car we will drive, and on what Caribbean island we will spend this year's vacation. Prosperity spoils us quickly and causes us to forget.

In Winston-Salem I did a lot of standing in welfare and social security lines with people, picking through burned-out houses, finding blankets, repairing windows, getting utility bills paid, trying to help people organize for a better future. Winston-Salem fixed on my consciousness a perspective I will never relinquish.

The stories in this section come mostly from the lives of people in Eleventh Street Bottom.

Five Loaves and Two Fish

The odor would be etched permanently in my memory. Few things penetrate like the reek of a burned-out house. It comes at you from every side, assaulting all your senses. Charred rubble, exuding this vicious smell.

It is a miracle all the people got out. Odessa, the teenage daughter, woke up and smelled smoke. Had the good sense to start screaming. Got everyone out in a few moments. Much longer and they would have all been cremated. Odessa did well.

But everything they owned is ruined. The front room sofa sends puffs of soot into the air with the slightest movement. The refrigerator has partially melted, no longer a faded white but now soot black. The food in the kitchen cabinet has been roasted. Clothes that hung in the closet have disintegrated to ash on the floor. Ugly. Sickening. I have never walked through a burned-out house before. I had not realized the indelible impression it leaves.

The family consists of Mama, Odessa, the teenage daughter, and two younger boys, Tim and Ricky. We are all picking through to see if anything remains. No one can be sure how it started, but they suspect it was an electrical cord. It started in the living room and spread toward the back.

The fire department is still here, the red light on top of the truck casting an eerie, revolving glow that swings over everything.

And now a television crew has arrived. This is a six o'clock headline in a town our size. But something is strange. The TV crew is not interested in interviewing Mama on what the family will do now that everything is gone. The TV people have pulled one of the firemen out on the sidewalk, and they are talking about, of all things, the family Bible. The fireman is leafing through Mama's big Sunday school Bible showing how, even in a fire this hot, just the edges of the pages get singed, how you can still read it perfectly well. The reporter and the fireman marvel together. "Do you think it's a miracle," the reporter asks, "that God reaches down and protects the holy book?"

"I'm sure it is a miracle," the fireman says. "It happens over and over. Everything else burns, but the family Bible stays in good shape."

"God taking care of what's holy," the reporter suggests.

"Yeah, I think it is," the fireman replies.

This piece of inane trivia will appear on the six o'-clock news, not the fact that every rental house on this hillside is a seventy-year-old tinderbox waiting to explode—with three thousand residents who may not wake up and scream the way Odessa did.

"Ricky, run over to Aunt Jane's and tell her what's happened," Mama says to her younger son. "See if we can go up there for a a few days."

"We'll take you there, Ricky," says my working companion, Jimmie, "there's not much more to be found by sifting through this rubble." Ricky, Jimmie, and I get into my Volkswagen and drive the distance, seven or eight blocks.

"Aunt Jane" is not actually related to the family, just a friend of Mama's. She and her own family — husband, four children, and a grandmother — live in a house just a bit larger than the one that has burned, a five-room place with an old garage in back.

Ricky knocks at the door. Aunt Jane answers and ushers us all inside.

"We got burned out last night, Aunt Jane," Ricky says.

"Aw, naw!" says Aunt Jane, clutching her face in empathy. "Is everyone okay?"

"Dessie smelled the smoke and woke up. We all got out. But it sure scared us a good way. We all still croaking."

"Well, honey boy," Aunt Jane exclaims. "I am sure glad no one's hurt. What kin I do to help you?"

"Mama wants to know if we we can come up here and stay a while. Everything's pretty burned up, and we don't have much to go with right now."

"Lord's sake, Ricky! There's only four of you! You know you can come up here. We'll just edge over a little, and there'll be plenty of room. Gran'ma's used to having a lot of people around; this'll make her real happy. Uncle Ben brought us some fresh things out of his garden just yesterday, and we got enough food to feed the multitude. You run back down that hill and tell your mama to come on up here whenever she's ready.

"And, listen here, Ricky. Y'all don't go hangin' 'round that burned out place too long; it'll eat up your spirit, get you feeling all down and draggy. You come up here pretty soon. We're tickled to have you movin' in!"

Here is the miracle: not an unburned Bible, not the pages of a scorched book still readable, but a living manifestation of what is recorded in that book: five loaves and two fish that become more than enough. Seven people living in five rooms with plenty of space for four more. The willingness of a family that has nothing to share everything with a family that has even less. The common helpfulness that poor people often extend to other poor people.

"God taking care of what's holy"—yes, they certainly got that right, but "what's holy" has a different definition from what they thought.

I wish this could make the six o'clock news—Jesus feeding the multitude. The TV reporter left too early.

Seeing Things Differently Now

B.C. was what the 'hood called a jive artist. The coolest of the cool. Smart, intelligent, quick, sexy, and nineteen. His actual name was Earnest; B.C. stood for Bop City. He was full of himself, so much a neighborhood leader that he was accustomed to making his wishes known by no more than a glance. Everyone knew that before they took a position, they needed to find out what B.C. wanted.

B.C. did not live in Eleventh Street Bottom but in Boston, one of the Bottom's two rivals as the roughest neighborhood in the city. (The other was Happy Hill, a huge public-housing project.)

One summer night in 1968, there was a riot in Winston-Salem. It was big enough to make the national TV news, even though riots were not uncommon in that tumultuous year. Some friends phoned us from California to see if the whole town was going up in flames—TV reports have a way of painting trouble bigger than it is. We told our friends we were fine, that the rioting was confined to a two-block area between Boston and Eleventh

Street Bottom, and that it was not directly affecting the rest of the city.

My colleague, Jimmie, had been laying it hard on the teenagers of Eleventh Street Bottom that if there were riots in Winston-Salem, they should go immediately home and stay there — that if they were found hanging around, they could be arrested in a moment and charged with a lot of things they had nothing to do with, and that the penalties in such a time could be very, very harsh. Jimmie never knew what effect his sermon would have when the trouble came, but we were happy to read in the newspaper the next morning that of the seven or eight people arrested, not one was from the Bottom.

Not true of Boston, however. B.C.'s name was at the top of the list. He had thrown a Molotov cocktail into a Minit-Mart. He would tell me later, with considerable remorse, that he just got carried away trying to act cool among his friends, that he did it in the excitement of the moment. His account was believable, because basically he was a good-hearted kid.

It was an era when "law and order in the streets" was the favorite theme of many politicians. "Any of these hoodlums caught rioting," it was said, "should be locked up for a long time! No mercy!" B.C. got four years in the state penitentiary. He was thoroughly disgusted, partially with the current political climate but far more with himself for getting involved in this mess. Four years out of his life; what a stupid thing he had done. He appealed the harsh sentence but was denied.

After three years, B.C. became eligible for a prisoner-release program. Someone had to apply to be his sponsor by providing about five pages of personal information. After a background check, that person might qualify to take B.C. out of prison one Saturday each month. B.C. was to stay in the sponsor's presence at all times — no lapses whatever. Any transgression would kick in the additional three years of probation attached to his four-year sentence. I applied to be B.C.'s sponsor. After about six weeks, I was approved.

The state prison farm was thirty-five miles north of town in a rural location. I pulled into the parking lot at 9:55 A.M. on the first scheduled Saturday. After brief paperwork, we were ready to go. We had to have him back by seven o'clock that night.

As we motored down the road, he seemed very quiet for a while. I finally realized he was shell-shocked. "Trees! Highway! Homes! People! Children!" he exclaimed, "It seems like another world!" Three years is a long time.

We proceeded to Nancy's and my house for an early lunch. B.C. had great appreciation for home-cooked food. He and Nancy carried on a friendly conversation.

Our older son, Andy, was three that year. Andy affectionately labeled B.C. "A.B.C.Y.D.," a play on the alphabet Andy was beginning to learn. B.C. liked it, as did Andy.

After a few minutes of baseball on TV, B.C. was ready to go visiting. We hopped in the black Volkswagen and took off.

First came a circuit through downtown. B.C. wanted to see what was where now. Down Fourth Street across Market, Trade, Main — B.C. gaped. "I can't believe how different this place is! I'll have to start over learning my way around. This is a new place."

I really didn't see the change. Winston-Salem came across to me like a reserved, southern town that pretty much stayed the same forever. B.C. was seeing something I didn't see.

"607 West Nineteenth Street," he finally said. "That's where my best friend lives. He knows I'm coming." We headed for Boston.

"B.C., man, great to see you! How you doin'? Come on in," the huge figure of Tommy greeted him. B.C. went inside. I followed, because I was supposed to. I sat down quietly in a stuffed chair. "What's goin' on, man? Tell me about life in the clink. You starvin' for affection up there? What's happening?"

B.C. and Tommy carried on for a while. I listened and watched.

At length, Eddie arrived. More greetings: "B.C., man . . ."

And then Cecil. The room was getting crowded. It was a lively conversation, but B.C. had this way of remaining slightly cool, a touch above it all. He remembered well how to play the game.

Then Clarence arrived. Then Otto. The party was getting big, outgrowing the room. B.C. clearly maintained his status as the center.

Then someone made the fateful comment—I had known it was coming and was waiting—"Well, let's go out and do it, man! We don't have to hang around here all afternoon."

Someone else joined in, "Yeah, let's go see what's goin' on."

After the excitement of the idea was shared around the room, there was a pause for B.C. to respond. It became a longer pause than I wanted. Finally, B.C. spoke.

"I got to stick with my man over there," he said, glancing at me. His hesitation hinted that he was struggling. It was a struggle that I told myself was inevitable.

The whole room turned toward me: a lone honky thoroughly out of place. They had ignored me until now, but suddenly I occupied center stage.

I was the chain holding the proceeding back. They could have a great afternoon except for me. They all realized that.

I was not going to get into a discussion with them over bending the prison's leave policy. If B.C. decided to take off, he could do it. I wasn't going to stop him. He knew the rules as well as I did. He also knew the outcome. I sat silently waiting to see what would happen.

"Yeah, let's go make it happen, B.C." another voice chimed in.

"Yeah, com'on, man!" said another.

B.C. replied, this time more distinctly, more decisively, "I got to stick with my man over there!"

The authority had pronounced its verdict. "That's it," the group seemed to conclude. No one else urged.

I became aware, surprisingly, that I took on new status in the room: B.C.'s man! There was a touch of reverence, a flick of acclaim. I marveled at the subtle powers of leadership, how a single person can steer so many.

The conversation went on for another hour. Then B.C. announced that it was over. He and I had to leave.

Two or three of his friends actually came and shook my hand to thank me for bringing him out. I had definitely turned a corner.

"Next, to Mama's store," B.C. said as we got in the car. "She'll be shutting it down pretty soon."

Mama owned and operated the neighborhood grocery in Boston, about four blocks away. I had never met her before. As soon as I did, I knew where B.C. had come from. Ultimate cool! Savvy! Quick! Even one up on B.C. I loved relating to her because I didn't want to miss a single word.

She greeted him profusely: the return of the prodigal. She obviously loved him dearly. They talked for a while about cousins and aunts. At one point, she walked toward the back of the store to get something from her freezer. She beckoned me to follow, wanting to show me something. Suddenly, from behind a tall showcase at the back of the store, she wheeled and barked at B.C., "Naw! Naw, young man! You still gotta ask first." B.C. was quietly lifting a pack of cigarettes from her front counter stand.

"Forever my faithful Mama," he said, grinning.

"They're all gonna play straight in my store," she said, "no matter how old they get."

After several moments, the scene from earlier in the afternoon began to materialize again. An old friend walked in the door and greeted B.C., "B.C., man, how you doin'?" And another friend.

"Let's go do the scene!" one of them said, not aware of who I was at all.

"Yeah, let's go."

B.C. was more definitive this time: "I got to stick with my man over there."

"You mean he's gotta be with you all the time you're out?" one of them said, implying that this situation was worse than prison.

Suddenly, a voice as authoritative as any I have ever heard roared over the proceeding. "Yes, that's right!" declared Mama, "and you, sonny boy, ain't talkin' nobody out of it. I want my son back sooner rather than later!"

That ended that. Not another murmur.

We shut the store and went up to Mama's apartment to visit. She wanted us to stay for dinner, but there wasn't enough time for her to fix it. After one more turn through downtown, we routed by our house for a snack. By then, Andy was thoroughly enthralled with A.B.C.Y.D.

On the way back to the prison, as we drove along a desolate stretch, B.C., seemingly out of nowhere, commented, "You'd never believe how much money has been bet in there on whether I'll come back or not."

I did not reply, trying to sense if he was kidding. Then I said, "I think we settled that earlier."

He paused, teasing me. "I think we did!" he finally declared.

"You know, B.C., you keep talking about how much everything has changed. I think I know what's changed," I said.

"Yeah, I think we both know," he said. "Twenty-three is a lot different from nineteen."

"You got it," I replied.

That was the first of several Saturdays out B.C. would enjoy before his full release a year later.

The last time I saw him, about a year later, he was at a conference of area social action organizations at Wake Forest University, standing up front during a worship service helping serve communion. I sat there remembering his history. He looked pretty good in his role as a pastor.

Don't Say It

Miss Jessie was the neighborhood matriarch. Now in her early seventies, she had lived in Eleventh Street Bottom for four decades. Her small, second-floor apartment was at the busy intersection of Eleventh and Dunleith Streets.

From her front porch she had raised generations of neighborhood children, warning them in her gutteral roar to dodge the buses and the hot-rods, scolding them for picking on the smaller kids, tying their shoes and zipping their coats, feeding them if they looked hungry, sending them home when it was time for them to get off the streets. No matter how much noise was happening in the Bottom, you always heard Miss Jessie over everything else.

Even as "her children" grew to be full-sized young adults who frequented the corner beer hall, they were careful never to cross Miss Jessie, because they somehow retained through life the primitive sense of what a serious matter doing so would have been.

The Bottom was her life. She knew its families, its history, its customs, its virtues, its sorrows, its soul.

She was a walking compendium of information on people. I once asked her about Mr. Talmadge Lewis, the old gentleman who lived at the far end of her block and carried a large Bible everywhere he went. "Where did Mr. Lewis get religion?" I inquired. She quoted date, location, event, preacher's name, and what he had said to claim Mr. Lewis.

She worked part time at Goodwill Industries on the sorting line. She sat beside a conveyor belt trying to match odd items, like socks or gloves. It was something she could make a little money at without being on her feet all the time.

The mayor's office did not dare ignore one of her phone calls. "Get someone down here to clean up the rubble washed down the hill by that storm last night! One of these little children is gonna get hurt playing in that trash!" The garbage truck would show up later that morning.

Very little happened in the Bottom that did not meet with Miss Jessie's approval. On one hot summer afternoon after a rainstorm, I stood on her front porch and watched a rat make its way along the dirt sidewalk beside her street. Miss Jessie waited for it to get in range and then, with nearly pinpoint accuracy, hurled an empty Pepsi bottle at it, knowing the bottle wouldn't break when it hit the moist dirt. Not expecting anything from above, the rat never saw it coming. It thudded two feet from the rat's head. Momentarily stunned, the rat darted this way and that for a moment, finally running for the alley across the street. It disappeared amid several trash cans. Miss Jessie had missed, but there was no doubt in that rat's mind that he had trespassed on holy ground. I was sure he would not make that mistake again.

Her pride in the neighborhood could be excessive. One morning we were loading a bus with children for a trip to the Reynolda science center near Wake Forest University. "Miss Jessie's playing cop!" one of the adults reported. Miss Jessie was standing at the bus door examining each child to see that they were dressed nicely enough to represent the neighborhood in the more affluent end of town. If she felt they were not, she would send them back home to put on something nicer. I did not like her vetoing children, but I had to honor her sense of pride.

Through four decades she had fought for the good of that neighborhood's children. She could "put on the beg act before the bigwigs" if she wanted something for the kids, or she could protest all the way to the police chief if she felt their treatment was unfair. Children would remain her cause as long as she could get around.

"The hardest, bitterest thing," she said to me one day, "is the broken promise. The antipoverty people come in here and wave a lot of money around, blow a lot of horns up and down the street, and promise how they're gonna make things better. And there's a lot of activity, a lot of people running this way and that, and a lot of meetings and a lot of big talk. But don't nothing get better.

"And the Black Panthers come in here. And they go around wearing them black leather coats and black armbands, and knocking on people's doors and making speeches and passing out leaflets, and promising how they're gonna make things better. But don't nothing get better.

"And then the politicians come in here, and they go around smiling and grinning and slipping a nip here and a dollar bill there, and they shake hands and joke and talk about Aunty's grandmother, and the new streetlights and cleaning up the creek, and about how everything's gonna get better. But don't nothing get better.

"And then the preachers come through here, and they're carrying them big thick Bibles, and standing on the street corner preaching 'bout the kingdom, and praying them heavenly prayers, and telling stories about people that turned from their evil ways and got saved, and instructing everyone on how they ought to live, and taking up offerings, and promising how they're gonna make everything better. But don't nothing get better.

"Son, learn it from me right now, if you ain't gonna do it, don't say it!"

It was one of the finest sermons I have ever heard. Spoken to politicians who make speeches, to lovers who say marriage vows, to pin-striped business executives who sign contracts, to advertisers who make commercials, to ministers who preach sermons — to all of us who relate to children: "If you ain't gonna do it, don't say it." Perform what you promise! Make your words have substance! A world built on anything less is a fraud.

Friends of a Different Sort

Tootie was a middle-aged woman who lived in Eleventh Street Bottom with her teenage son, Melvin (nicknamed Slick), and her daughter, Charonda, who was in her early twenties. They occupied one of the nicer homes in the neighborhood: six rooms, well maintained, a bit off to itself, with grass in the yard and a chain-link fence around the property.

Although Tootie's formal education had ended with high school, she was nevertheless sharp and discerning. Virtually nothing got by her. Slick would pass through the front room, and Tootie, without even looking up, would comment in a very even voice, "I told you to get rid of those nasty things," referring to the three cigarettes carefully hidden in his shirt pocket. Slick would blush, grin, and toss out the cigarettes. You could tell by the smile that he was very fond of his mother.

Tootie picked up immediately on humor. When the conversation turned funny, she was in the middle. A touch quiet and understated most of the time, she nevertheless had a very pleasant, joshing style.

There was something we never found out about Tootie. She had no steady job we could see. Her children were too old for her to draw child-welfare checks, and she suffered no disability. Perhaps her ex-husband sent her money, but it was doubtful. How did she live better than most others?

Whenever the neighborhood community organization, in which she was active, would gather itself together to visit the mayor or the board of aldermen with a cause, Tootie would defer: "Naw, that's not a place I need to be. Y'all go on, and I'll hear about it when you get back." People downtown knew her, but she wanted to

stay clear. We wondered if she owned a beer hall or perhaps ran a numbers game. We never found out.

Pat was a member of my house church. A Smith College
graduate, Pat's husband taught neurology at Bowman
Gray School of Medicine. They lived in a large home on
a shaded street in a beautiful area of Winston-Salem called
Buena Vista.

Pat was an extremely talented woman. In addition to
raising four young children, she played roles in local theater performances. Her backyard, which wandered down
an incline among trees, ferns, rocks, terraces, and flowers, became my picture of the Garden of Eden. She
spent hours there. She also read prolifically and carried
on an active social life among medical school faculty
friends and others.

Pat had joined the house church early, coming out of
a large downtown congregation that didn't challenge her
much. She agreed with our founding philosophy that the
church needed to take a serious role in the antipoverty
effort. She offered heart and soul to the task.

One evening the East Eleventh Street Community Association was discussing ways to earn money. A young
Winston-Salem State College student, Ron, who lived
just outside the Bottom, commented, "You know those
brightly colored African shirts called dashikis? They're
becoming really popular now, and y'all could earn a ton
if you would make some. Good ones are hard to find."

Tootie thought for a moment, "Yeah, we could do that."
Her niece, Betty, agreed.

Thus was launched the East Eleventh Street Sewing
Cooperative. Someone found some cheap used sewing
machines. A sewing room was set up on the second floor

of an old store area. Tootie and Betty organized about eight neighborhood women. Several of my house church members joined in. Three days each week they would get together and manufacture dashikis. The cooperative began turning out two or three dozen every week.

An old storefront was procured downtown. It became the Dashiki Shop, where youngsters from all over the city came to sample this latest fashion. Sales went really well. The East Eleventh Street Community Association began, for the first time, amassing a significant amount of money in its treasury.

The most remarkable part of the project, however, was not the money. From the beginning, Tootie and Pat had been the two minds at the head of it all. They would travel together each day to a fabric shop to buy the next day's materials. They would lay out designs and give instructions on how garments were to be made. (Pat says Tootie "taught me how to think about cloth.") They would assign particular dashikis to specific workers and oversee the quality of the work. They found a company in New York that marketed beautiful African block-print materials and began ordering these materials by the boxload. Tootie and Pat made the business go. Tootie knew a great deal about sewing and about the people of Eleventh Street Bottom, and Pat, besides owning a car, knew about running an organization.

Before long, Tootie and Pat came to realize that they had become good friends. How likely was this: a middle-aged ghetto resident who would soon be a grandmother and a blond doctor's wife with preschool children? They were from different races, entirely different lifestyles. But they discovered that they identified with and understood each other and shared common interests and concerns. And, most important, they liked each other.

Pat appreciated the open window onto ghetto life: the opportunity to see what life was actually like in a neighborhood the rest of the city thought was dangerous, to discern the social customs that connected low-income people. The relationship enabled her to step outside her normal mode and genuinely expand her world. Tootie, I think, enjoyed having a very bright graduate of a prestigious college as her eager student. She loved sharing insights.

Few of Pat's acquaintances in her end of town could comprehend. She would try to tell about having a close friend who was a lifelong resident of Eleventh Street Bottom, but no one seemed to value the insights she had gained.

In 1969 there was a riot early one evening in a neighborhood adjacent to Eleventh Street Bottom. About two blocks of stores and businesses were looted and fire bombed. The next morning, anxiety ran high across the city. A store owner in an affluent west end shopping center told me that he had heard that gangs of low-income youth were arming themselves to invade the rest of the city that night and that he was going to prepare himself to defend his property. A man in Eleventh Street Bottom told me that he had heard that gangs of shotgun-wielding white folks planned to invade Boston and the Bottom that night in retaliation for the riots.

It was sewing co-op morning, and Pat made her way past the riot area toward the co-op building. As she drove down one street, a man began yelling at her and shaking his hand at her car. He apparently recognized that she was from outside the neighborhood. The incident scared her briefly but not enough to turn her back. She had no further problem. Relating the story to a couple of friends, however, she got a horrified response, "What were you doing down there?"

From that time forward, Pat just kept quiet among her friends. "I lived a double life," she says, "this incredibly meaningful friendship that no riot could stop but that I could not even mention on my side of town."

Pat very tentatively invited Tootie and her niece, Betty Squire, to lunch at Pat's house. She wondered if they would be put off by the affluence, and she did not want to sacrifice their friendship. But she also wanted to be authentic. They stayed several hours and had a wonderful time.

Two years later, when Pat and her husband were transplanting themselves for a year of study in California, Tootie used her house to host a neighborhood going-away party for Pat. Amid fruit punch and pound cake, the East Eleventh Street Sewing Cooperative remembered all their experiences together. At the high moment of the party, Tootie presented Pat with a personal gift: a dashiki, complete with a note signed by all the co-op members. The note authorized Pat, a white woman, to wear the dashiki. To this day Pat still considers it one of the most endearing gifts she has ever received.

For years I have tried to get low-income people and upper-middle income people to talk to each other. The modern city does us an enormous disservice by separating the two so that they never meet. It creates a natural breeding ground for fear and prejudice and unfounded stories.

Each group has a great deal to learn from the other. The education runs in both directions. Tootie and Pat were the shining example of what can be.

Something Wrong with Bill

Bill was born in South Carolina, the third child in a large family. At first he seemed like a normal baby, but a routine medical exam not far into his life sent a shock wave through the family: "There is something wrong with Bill." That "something wrong" was cerebral palsy. Bill's illness was quite involved. His mind worked perfectly well, but his body was significantly contorted. He would spend virtually his whole life in a wheelchair.

I first met Bill while he was living at Goodwill Industries in Winston-Salem. He had a very nicely appointed room in their dormitory, and he wrote public-relations materials to advertise their work. A couple in our house church brought him with them to one of our meetings.

Bill was a likable fellow, intelligent, interested, and quick. He caught the spirit of our organization and took only a short time to become one of us. He could not physically join the work we were doing — rehabilitating old houses, operating a youth service center, working with a sewing cooperative — but he could join our extensive deliberations over the best ways and the not-so-good ways to try to help people, and he could participate fully in our Bible studies. Bill and his wheelchair became a standard part of almost everything we did.

Somewhere earlier in his adult life, Bill had made a fateful decision. Someone had convinced him that there was a medical operation that could at least partially cure cerebral palsy, a brain procedure that could improve his condition. Bill had become convinced — I don't know who did the convincing — that it would work. He had agreed to let someone open up his brain and perform the work. It had been a vast mistake. The procedure had created no improvement at all (although at least it had done no mental damage), but it had left a large caved-in area in Bill's skull. His head looked like someone had taken a scoop out of one side. His hair had grown back as cover, but the damage remained quite apparent.

Bill had a consuming passion to be autonomous. He appreciated the room Goodwill was providing for him, and he wanted to continue the public-relations work he was doing for them. But he basically disliked living there. He found that he lived day and night, shoulder to shoulder, with a great variety of people he had neither chosen nor particularly liked. Some of them were loud and boisterous, some devious and scheming, some simply unpleasant and demeaning to him. If he had been able to take care of himself better, he could have spent more time in his room by himself. But, as it was, he had to live among all of them all the time. He grew weary of the surroundings.

And Bill also struggled mightily with depression. There would be periods when his despair would be all consuming. Despite his efforts, despite his successes, despite his hopes, he would give in to the inner voice that told him it was all futile, that he would never get anywhere worthwhile in his life. That voice was frequent and pervasive. A number of times I and others sat with Bill through his depressive bouts, trying to keep him from wanting to kill himself, trying to help him find a glimmer of hope.

Bill, as much as any person I have ever known, embodied within himself both an enormous will to move forward, to achieve, and a dark cloud that told him it would never happen. He struggled hard to feel great, and he was perpetually tempted to feel rotten. Really up, really down: Bill would be somewhere in that range. The ups were inspiring, the downs were horrible. It was his life.

Bill concocted elaborate plans to move himself into his own private apartment. The idea seemed beyond all realism to most of us who knew him, but Bill pecked away. He found someone willing to pledge some money. He found a suitable rental unit with a landlord who was willing. He found an interior designer who worked with him in developing the plans to fit his daily needs. In the middle of it all, he tried to commit suicide by taking a vast overdose of someone else's pain pills.

After months of effort, Bill's apartment was fully set up. Bill left the Goodwill Industry dormitory for his new home. It was wonderful. Everything could be reached from a sitting position: refrigerator, stove, ceiling pull chains, bookshelves. There was an electric can opener Bill could manipulate completely with one hand. The medicine cabinet in the bathroom was at half height. Special buttons locked and unlocked doors. Rotating shelves in the kitchen cabinets presented to Bill what he could select for dinner. In the mirrors I saw my knees. Bill could use everything with minimal difficulty.

Just after he moved into his new place, our family departed from Winston-Salem.

One night about two years later, we, in Columbus, Ohio, were watching the eleven o'clock television news. The teaser for the next story after a commercial break was, "President Carter presents national handicapped person of the year award." I thought I spotted a familiar figure in the accompanying picture. Sure enough, when the full story came on, there sat Bill, sunken head and all, a huge smile on his face, in the Rose Garden of the White House, with President Jimmy Carter presenting him a plaque. Out of all the handicapped people in the country, Bill had been selected that year as the one who had achieved the most notable accomplishments. He had really won with that apartment. The whole world was proud of him that night.

Not too long afterward, Bill died. I never asked anyone how, because I suspected I might not want to know.

A man of incredible victory, a man of always-lurking defeat—wrapped in a single, less-than-perfectly-formed body. I guess he was an exaggerated picture of all of us.

The Marriage of Two Worlds

Sarah was a young social worker, a graduate of the University of North Carolina School of Social Work. She had grown up in a small town in eastern North Carolina, in the sand hill region. She looked to be on the move, out to accomplish, assertive — but not on her own behalf. Her cause was justice and opportunity among the poor people who were her clients. She had a well-nurtured social conscience and intended to live her life following its calls.

It was also apparent, from observing Sarah, that her family had occupied a position of status on the eastern North Carolina social ladder. She bore a grace that did not come from potato farming. The soft manner, the elegant style — touches were still evident in her, even though she was now pointing her life in a different direction.

Her parents had not only been socially prominent but were also Quakers. They believed in the ideals of social equality and universal human dignity. They had taught their daughter that all people are to be cherished and honored before God. Sarah was a next-generation embodiment of their Quaker values.

Cedric was a product of the Brooklyn streets. He was big, physically imposing, possibly 6'3" and 250 pounds. He had never had the advantage of higher education but had learned a lot from life's varied offerings. He maintained a dark black beard that gave him a slightly wise and discerning look, and he had deep, friendly eyes. He read newspapers, attended seminars, and kept up with books. Cecil was usually considered an authority by younger people because he had a take on situations that was often unique and worthwhile.

Early in his adult life, Cedric had been a New York City delivery truck driver. Then he had become a shop worker, and after that a union organizer. He worked the streets, mingling with people, rallying members, encouraging the rank and file. He had brought those skills south to work in the newly emerging antipoverty program.

He had a keen eye for racial injustice—he had experienced it many times—and he was committed to finding a new day for his brothers and sisters.

Sarah and Cedric called me one day to ask if I would perform their marriage. I was surprised. I knew them both, but I had not put them together in my mind.

I told them I would be delighted! This would be my first white-black marriage, and I frankly looked forward to the experience. I was honored that they had selected me, figuring that they both had pastoral contacts back home.

They planned to get married on a Saturday morning at a Quaker retreat center outside Greensboro. It sounded like a lovely setting, simple but with a touch of natural grace. There would be six bridesmaids and six ushers. Most of the bridesmaids would be her friends, and most of the ushers would be his. Dress would be formal: the men would wear tuxedos. Sarah and Cedric wanted their "really nice" ceremony in this simple setting. We set all the plans.

The day came. The retreat center lodge looked charming amid nature's early-June elegance. Lovely flowers decorated the main lodge room, and chairs had been set out in neat rows. The people seemed happy; pleasant conversation flowed. It was a very good morning, and we were all enjoying ourselves.

As the hour grew near, the ushers began seating guests. The ushers were definitely not accustomed to wearing tuxedos, but they looked splendid. Each would walk down the aisle with a woman on his arm with all due formality, just as they had been taught. They would walk back up the aisle to the rear in a swinging, jiving, half–dance step, perfect for relieving their anxiety and for entertaining the audience.

The bridesmaids had assembled and were ready in a rear dressing room. The groom's party was ready on a side porch.

About eight minutes before the ceremony, the schedule was put on hold. Cedric's mother had not arrived. She had flown in from New York the night before — we knew that — so there was no worry. But there would be a short delay, because we definitely did not want to carry on without her. No one was in a hurry, and it didn't really matter.

Standing in the yard outside the lodge, I observed for the first time Sarah's mother (her father had died several years before). Sarah's mother was an erect, dignified woman, dressed in a turquoise suit. She bore fully the eastern North Carolina elegance. Sarah had told me, however, about the quiet struggle going on in her mother, and I saw it clearly now.

She rather nervously moved back and forth across the front porch, gazing here and there. I could tell that her Quaker values were doing battle with what she knew her eastern North Carolina friends would think of this moment. Conviction was at conflict with "back home." This wedding was right, but it had not occurred to her through the years that the person who would ask her to affirm it would be her own daughter.

With two minutes left before the wedding time, a Lincoln Continental turned into the driveway. It proceeded up the road and entered the yard. It turned a large circle and pulled to a stop near the porch. A man emerged from the driver's seat. He came around the car and opened the opposite door. Out stepped Cedric's mother. She, too, bore a dignity that befitted her, but it spoke Brooklyn rather than the plantation South. Hers was another place, another culture.

Sarah's mother hesitated. Cedric's mother hesitated. For an instant they did not seem to have decided what to do. Then, they advanced toward each other. They met in a warm embrace that would have befitted lifelong friends. They stood for several moments, their worlds greeting.

Conviction set aside convention. The future triumphed over the past. They had struggled with the beast, and it had not prevailed. I thought I saw the Holy City descending from heaven.

Sarah's mother clasped Cedric's mother's hand. They walked triumphantly up the porch steps into the lodge.

The wedding went beautifully, with tears and laughter. Sarah was a lovely bride, Cedric a handsome groom. The ushers grinned; the bridesmaids smiled happily.

My only regret was that I never found out what was going on in Cedric's mother's mind, what her friends back home were saying. It would have been intensely interesting to compare the two.

"A Gift from the Lord"

The Urban Renewal Office announced that a large grant had been procured to rehabilitate owner-occupied low-income housing in Winston-Salem. Grants would be available to do basic repairs. It was an excellent program. Low-income home owners, who made up about 15 percent of the ghetto population, tended to keep up their properties very devotedly, but they usually lacked the capital to do large work. This grant would repair roofs, furnaces, foundations, drainage systems, and other basics.

The local TV station immediately sent a crew to the Urban Renewal Office. From that interview they gleaned all the essential data: 90 percent federal money, 10 percent state money; to qualify, a home owner had to have less than two thousand dollars in yearly income and cash assets under five thousand dollars; and so on.

The TV station then sent its crew to interview the local politicians. "Oh, yes, this is a wonderful program we have procured for Winston-Salem. It came from a cooperative partnership between Washington, Raleigh, and those of us working hard here in Forsyth County. It happened because economic need in this country transcends partisan politics; we all worked together. We take deep satisfaction in what we have been able to do. It is a wonderful thing for our city." In other words, the politicians preened. It is, of course, the favorite mode of politicians in public view.

Finally the TV station sent a crew to Eleventh Street Bottom, specifically to talk to Mr. Hudson, a seventy-eight-year-old man who would be one of the first beneficiaries of the grant.

The young reporter, neatly attired from the L. L. Bean catalog (if there was such a thing back then), was trying hard to appear professional. It wasn't easy. He was interviewing a man fifty years his elder who had long since decided what was important in life.

"Mr. Hudson, you will be one of the first people helped by this grant. What are you thinking right now?"

Mr. Hudson's eyes sparkled. He broke into a deeply contented smile. "It's a gift from the Lord, son, a gift from the Lord."

"You're slated for a new hot-water heater and a new roof. Will that improve your life?"

"Oh, yes, definitely!" Mr. Hudson gained even more enthusiasm. "It's a gift from the Lord, a gift straight from the Lord."

"Most of the money is coming through a federal grant. Do you think this represents a significant commitment from the government to helping needy people like you?"

"I think it's wonderful." Mr. Hudson was nearly dancing by now, his whole body radiating his feeling. "It's marvelous, a gift from the Lord, a gift from the Lord!"

The reporter was obviously getting frustrated. He wanted a statement from this man and was struggling hard to formulate a question that would lead somewhere he wanted to go.

"Mr. Hudson, why do you prefer to stay in your own house rather than moving into one of the new apartments Urban Renewal is building?"

"Because here I can live exactly the way I want, without bothering anyone. I'm free!" He sounded like he had just passed through the waters of the Red Sea. "It's a gift from the Lord, son, a gift from the Lord."

"Mr. Hudson, how will you express your appreciation for this help? Do you intend to write a letter to the mayor?"

With this question, the rapture nearly arrived. Mr. Hudson never pondered his reply. There was only one possibility. "I will walk on my two feet to church Sunday, the way I always do. I will bow on my knees in solemn prayer, and I will give thanks before the great God of heaven and earth, the Lord of grace who has brought to me this magnificent gift. I will sing praises to God's holy name, and I will live in eternal thanksgiving. It's a gift from the Lord, a gift from the Lord!"

The reporter, by now thoroughly perplexed, stopped. He was not going forward with any more of this. He could not get Mr. Hudson to take part in his world—he had certainly tried. And he clearly was not willing to take part in Mr. Hudson's world: it would not have been professional. He closed up his equipment and left, thoroughly frustrated by the experience.

I felt sorry about the narrow confine in which he was forcing himself to live: within the limits of what he considered "real." He could not venture into the much larger and richer world of what human beings believe.

It was debilitating, true poverty.

Cluckers

The call came about four o'clock one afternoon. Mrs. Arthur, a forty-eight-year-old woman who lived several blocks away, had been evicted. The constable had knocked on her door that morning, served the final legal papers for nonpayment of rent, entered the house—which was no longer "her property"—and had set all her belongings outside, leaving an empty dwelling that he had bolted against her return. It was a rude way to do business, but it was the way business was done. The constable had performed this duty many times before, and he would do it again.

"We better go get us a truck fast, before the rental office closes," said my colleague, Jimmie. I agreed. An hour later we had purchased the use of a half-ton truck for a day and were pulling up in front of Mrs. Arthur's former residence.

The scene was a shambles. Stove, refrigerator, dressers, and beds had been set out on the sidewalk in front of the house. Several smaller pieces of furniture were in the front yard. Clothes, shoes, carpets, kitchenware, clocks, a radio, pictures, papers, and trinkets had been thrown out the windows and were lying in heaps around the side. A large trunk from the kitchen had landed in the backyard, its contents spilling across the ground. Even the window shades had been taken down and were unrolling off the back porch. I was overwhelmed by how much stuff can come out of a four-room dwelling.

There was an unwritten code that governed the neighborhood. When someone got evicted, they had until sundown to claim their belongings and get them secured. No one else was to fool around with the things as long as the sun was visible.

After the sun dropped, however, the neighbors were welcome to snoop through and see if there was anything they wanted. They called it "cluckin," a name drawn from what chickens do with corn spread across a barnyard. It could turn into quite a social event, a treasure hunt with flashlights and lots of hilarity. The evictee did not expect to find anything left by the next morning.

I never once saw this custom violated in Eleventh Street Bottom. To take undue advantage of a neighbor who had been evicted would have been considered the lowest kind of human behavior.

"We got about two hours," Jimmie said, checking the sun. "Better get to work." Our plan was to load all of Mrs. Arthur's things into the half-ton, keep them overnight, and store them the next morning at her sister's house some distance away.

It was rat work. Not knowing exactly what Mrs. Arthur would or wouldn't want, we tried to preserve everything. The appliances were heavy and the furniture hard to load up the truck ramp. Jimmie and I were working hard and feeling the pressure. It would be a tight squeeze to get it all in by sundown. We kept up the pace.

Then, from around the side of the house, we heard whistling and singing. "Boy, oh boy; boy, oh boy. See what ya git when ya don't pay your rent. Ain't this something! Doodads all over the yard. Everywhere. Mercy me. Better to keep up the rent payments."

Jimmie commented, "The cluckers are early." Two slick-looking jive artists appeared, licking their chops, almost drooling over the pickings.

"Mercy me," went on one of them. "Just look at all the dandy stuff. You boys'll never get all this packed away 'fore dusk falls. Some good lookin' thangs here. Mercy me."

"It's what happens to you when you don't git that li'l rent check in on time," carried on the other. "Mr. Constable—big, stern Mr. Constable—he comes through your door and throws it all out in the yard. What a pity! What a pity! But he don't have pity on nobody."

"We'd better move faster," said Jimmie.

Then the first man continued, "Y'all never get this loaded by sundown. C'm'on, Eddie, let's help these dudes do the job. This poor lady shouldn't lose all her stuff."

For the next ninety minutes Jaybird and Eddie added their strength to ours, hauling furniture, lifting it onto the truck, packing it securely. We regarded them suspiciously at first but soon realized they were for real. For all the talk, they were jewels. When the job was finished, we thanked them sincerely. They acted as if it had not been much, and they left.

I try in most circumstances not to anticipate, based on how people look or act, the response I am going to get from them. I entirely misjudged this one.

George's Little Jump Shot

I worked my way around the edge of the asphalt playground basketball court, camera in hand. One or two photographs had presented themselves, but not much. I was selective, waiting my time.

The teams were pickup, high school kids from Eleventh Street Bottom. Eddie, Lomax, June, Willie, Vincent, Theoddus, and a couple of others. They played hard, seriously, as if this might be someone's future, or as if they were trying to impress girls. But they were also friends, so they didn't play too hard, too seriously. The point was to have fun, which they were.

I knelt at the side of the court. "Time-out!" I heard. George, who had just hit a basket from the corner, was taking the ball out in the backcourt. He said it again, this time waving his hand slightly: "Time-out." The game paused.

George walked over and knelt be beside me, a very serious look on his face. I didn't have any idea what he was getting ready to say. Was I bothering his concentration? Was he afraid I'd get run over? Did he, for some unknown reason, not want me taking pictures of the game? Was there some imagined injustice in the shots I had selected? It was a mystery. I waited to see.

I looked at him, "What's up, George?"

He paused. Then he looked at me quite seriously and said, rather quietly, "Reverend Chatham, would you mind taking a picture of my little jump shot? Just as I get up in the air and the ball leaves my hand—can you get a shot right at the peak? I'd really appreciate it if you would."

George had not been able to accomplish much in his short life. A high school junior, not particularly smart. Not the best looking kid on the block. Cool, but not nearly the coolest. A couple of nice-looking shirts, but no great wardrobe. No awards, no achievements, no notable victories. Not even the best player on this court. People liked George, but he was hardly special—just part of the neighborhood.

What George wanted was, just for one moment, to *be someone,* to be a bit special, to occupy the limelight.

His little jump shot was the closest he had been able to come so far, and he wanted a picture of it so he could remember it better.

That is, when all is said and done, the same thing most of us want most of the time: just to be someone. It's really fairly simple.

"George, I'll be glad to photograph you," I said. "Next time you go up, I'll be there. You just make sure you hit it so it won't be a fraud."

His face warmed. He agreed he would. I still have a copy of that photograph.

Let's Find Us a Poor Family

The East Eleventh Street Community Association was holding its December meeting. Around the room sat a variety of neighborhood residents.

There was Mr. T, who had worked on the leaf line at R. J. Reynolds for forty-four years before being given a gold watch at his retirement. Reynolds had no workers' union, and its black employees were paid barely more than a subsistence wage.

There was Hazel, mother of eleven children, all of whom lived in a four-room frame house on Dunleith Street. Hazel's son, Billy, had become a neighborhood celebrity when he built a wooden race car in his uncle's garage and entered it in the local soapbox derby. The whole neighborhood had turned out to cheer him. He lost in the first heat, but it was the only time anything like this had ever happened, and the neighborhood was no less proud.

There was Jimmie, the young stock clerk in the small neighborhood grocery store. Jimmie earned about half the minimum wage because the store was not classified as an interstate business.

There was Lawrence, Jimmie's younger brother, who was already married and living with his pregnant wife in one side of a three-room duplex ($9.50 a week rent).

There was Miss Jessie, the neighborhood matriarch, who worked part time on the sorting line at Goodwill.

There was Sharanda, who drew Aid to Families with Dependent Children for her three young ones.

There was Mr. Talmadge, who lived alone in a run-down two-room apartment and carried his Bible everywhere he went.

There was Mrs. McCoy, the acknowledged neighborhood authority on making a little food stretch a long way.

There was Mrs. Perkins, who had had her electric power cut off the week before because she couldn't pay her bill.

There was Betty, who was studying one course at a time to get a two-year business degree so that she could move herself and her two children, Dimitris and Meatball, out of the public housing project.

There was Mrs. Johnson, who had not been able to buy her food stamps that week because her retirement check had been delayed in the mail and she could not come up with her matching 12 percent.

These members of the East Eleventh Street Community Association had gathered to plan the association's Christmas party.

"Pink lemonade, that looks festive!" Mrs. McCoy had suggested.

"Yes, and we can string popcorn to hang around the room," said Mrs. Perkins.

"And let's have the children make Christmas cards," continued Betty. "They can deliver them around the neighborhood. All the older people will like that."

"Yeah," said Mrs. Johnson, "and we can get Mr. T's sister to lead us in singing Christmas carols. She has a wonderful voice."

"Yeah," said Jimmie, "and let's bob for apples. Mr. Jack's got an unopened bag of them in the back of the grocery store, and he might let us have a few."

The plans flowed fast and furiously. Everyone liked a Christmas party, and no one was without an idea.

And then, as the suggestions waned slightly, Hazel spoke up, not with any flourish but simply to add one more idea. You had to be listening carefully to notice it. "Let's everyone chip in whatever money we can, and let's find us a poor family and fix them a Christmas basket."

Had she really said that: "Let's find us a poor family?" Did I hear her correctly? I was stunned. I sat gazing at Hazel, wondering what sort of mental arithmetic brought her to a comment like that. How we view life is completely relative. The one thing for certain is that few of us want to see ourselves at the bottom of the ladder.

Thou Shalt Receive No Pile

I had a phone call one day from my Uncle Gurdie, a tobacco farmer on a two hundred–acre farm outside East Bend, North Carolina. Uncle Gurdie — married to my father's sister until her death — had been selling his flue-cured tobacco crop at the Winston-Salem auction for fifty years. He was a hardworking man who rarely said much. When asked, "How are you, Gurdie?" his stock reply was, "Not too bad; can't complain," which he never did. Gurdie looked thoroughly at home in overalls, work shirt, and boots and thoroughly out of place in a jacket and tie, which he wore over a clean pair of overalls on Sundays and for brief "business doings" in town.

He always gave me the impression of being a tower of sturdiness, one of those people who moves through life carrying out quietly but diligently whatever the years ask of him. Even in his late eighties he still raised a pretty decent crop of tobacco. I am sure that in painting "American Gothic," Grant Wood had Uncle Gurdie as his model.

Some of my most vivid memories from childhood are of riding Uncle Gurdie's mule, picking dried corn off a cob and throwing it to Uncle Gurdie's chickens, bouncing around in Uncle Gurdie's haystack, eating watermelon in Uncle Gurdie's watermelon patch, and skimming rocks across Uncle Gurdie's pond. Aunt Nell always greeted our visits with a glass jar full of her huge homemade sugar cookies. Those are long-lasting memories that make childhood a pleasant thing to recall.

Uncle Gurdie called to ask if I would go with him to a lawyer's office over in the county seat. He was trying to work out a new will now that Aunt Nell had died and her affairs were finally settled, and he said to me, "I ain't always too smart when it comes to things like this. I just thought it might be good to have you come along." I assured him I would be happy to come.

On the appointed Saturday morning we met at the lawyer's office. The lawyer was in his late fifties, obviously skilled at his work but without the polish of a big city attorney. He apparently had many other Uncle Gurdies on his client list, because he handled himself with both professional grace and small-town familiarity.

"What can I do for you, Gurdie?" he queried as we settled into his modest plywood-paneled office.

"Thought I better get my affairs straightened up," Uncle Gurdie replied, removing from his overall pocket the will he had written some years before. The attorney studied it quickly. After a couple of questions, he suggested starting over since the old will no longer reflected what Uncle Gurdie seemed to have in mind.

He produced a long yellow legal pad and began to write. In one page we disposed of all of Uncle Gurdie's major assets: some savings here, some stock there, and his major property — 95 percent of everything Uncle Gurdie owned. That part was simple.

But then we reached the category called "household belongings," and at this point Uncle Gurdie became a different person. He sat up in his chair and took command. He had been planning this for years, and now was his opportunity to articulate it. He spoke in a straightforward, determined style very uncharacteristic of his usual deference. "I want all four of the heirs to gather at my place on a Saturday morning," he said. "I want all my household belongings carried out into the yard — every last shred; nothing left. And I want everything divided into four equal piles. I want all four heirs to examine all four piles carefully, together, and agree that they are all equal."

The poor lawyer was beginning to squirm, Lawyers turn blue inside over language like this. But Uncle Gurdie continued without noticing. "When everyone agrees that all four piles are equal, I want the heirs to draw straws to see who gets which one." (Drawing straws is an old southern version of casting lots.) "Now, when it's all done, if any one of the heirs starts grumbling and kicking up a fuss over which pile they got and how someone else's pile was better, the executrix is to exclude that heir from the inheritance right then and there — completely out — and the whole thing is to start over again with the household belongings divided into three equal piles."

I glanced at Uncle Gurdie, thinking to myself, "Dear uncle, you are about ten truckloads smarter than you give yourself credit for. You didn't need me here today. You know a lot more about human life than I do!"

My head danced with the ugly inheritance scenes this man must have seen in his eighty-eight-plus years. And he had obviously plotted for years how to keep his own death from creating another one.

"Thou shalt not covet," the tenth commandment says. Uncle Gurdie was creating his own postscript: "If thou dost, thou shalt receive no pile at all." Not bad for a sun-baked Yadkin Valley tobacco farmer.

Louisville, Kentucky

1977 to the Present

I s Louisville southern? That question is much de-
bated. There are significant ways in which Louisville
has not been southern.

Louisville's economy did not, as with most of the
South, grow primarily from farming. Located at a point
of portage on the Ohio River, in a region that tends to
be hilly and with soil that bears a heavy clay content, the
city's economic base has come more from trade and industry than from agriculture.

Louisville has a history of strong organized labor, very
unusual and very suspect in the South.

Much of the city's wealth came from bourbon distil-
leries, an industry that would not have been acceptable
in most of the South since alcohol has been publicly considered sin by the predominant southern religion.

Louisville has long had large populations of Catholics
and Jews, not at all typical of the South.

Louisville's leadership desegregated its public school
system soon after the Supreme Court decision of 1954,
without waiting for a court order.

Honey-dripping southern accents, prominent in Nashville and Birmingham, have almost never been found in
Louisville. There is a distinct mid-Kentucky dialect, definitely identifiable, but it did not come from the cotton
plantations.

In the past half century, the southernness of the entire South, especially its urban regions, has been vastly diluted by the invasion of national uniformity. Syndicated radio and television programs have drowned out local flavor. Thirty years ago, for example, one could drive through eastern Kentucky and tune, one after another, small-town radio stations that spent the day playing "on the other side of Jordan" music performed by local church choirs and country groups. Now eastern Kentucky radio is blanketed by commercial country-and-western straight out of Nashville and Dallas.

Nationwide chain stores and restaurants have replaced many of the hometown mom-and-pop establishments. In Louisville we live just off one of the few streets, Bardstown Road, where the restaurants and stores are not the same ones found in every shopping mall in America and where something unique can still show up on a shelf or a menu.

The federal interstate highway system has made the major roads of the entire nation look and drive alike. Corporate buyouts and high employee mobility have interchanged southerners with all varieties of Americans. The last half of the twentieth century has seen a strong trend toward making the South like everywhere else.

And yet most people who live here even for a short time recognize that Louisville at its heart is thoroughly and totally southern.

Its rhythms bear the friendly, soft-edged quality of the South. At four-way stops, for example, polite Louisvillians often defer their turns, creating momentary confusion and a stuttering stop-start dance before someone finally goes through.

I remember flying into a city north of here late one afternoon. I entered an airport cafeteria to eat dinner.

As I glanced over the food offerings, the server behind the counter scowled at me, "Make up your mind, mister, you're not the only one in line!" Eighteen hours later I sat down for lunch in a Louisville restaurant. The waitress sauntered over and said, "Good afternoon, honey. Have you found something on that menu that I can get for you?" The contrast was a snapshot of Louisville's southernness.

Many Louisville people have been here all their lives. I often hear people introducing themselves to one another by comparing the high schools and elementary schools they attended. Despite national mobility, noticeable numbers of Louisvillians have never lived anywhere else, or, if they have, they have come back.

In Louisville, identity is tied primarily to family. You are rarely a single human being: you are part of a network of parents, grandparents, brothers, sisters, cousins, nieces, and nephews—whether you like them all or not. They are a main factor in your life; you have to apologize if you don't have much to do with them. The right family connections in Louisville can make you automatically significant. If you lack family connections, you may never compensate for it.

The first rule for getting along in Louisville is to be nice. Don't offend! This edict transcends every other item on the human agenda. Being nice is vastly more important than being forthright or honest or smart or talented. It doesn't matter who you are, how successful you have been, what status you hold, or what mood you are in. You may be sublimating a universe of negative emotions, but if you wish to fit in Louisville, you need to come across as nice.

I once served on the selection committee for an Old Testament professor at Louisville Presbyterian Theological Seminary. One candidate who came to town was internationally renowned in the field, a seasoned veteran of both scholarship and teaching. We on the selection committee interviewed him for a couple of hours, digging through his views on the world, his views on the Bible, his views on theological education. We took a break.

I walked out into hallway of the seminary administration building. The receptionist, a person I knew fairly well, caught my eye and said abruptly, "We don't want him."

"We don't want whom? What are you talking about?" I asked, drawing closer.

"We don't want that man you're interviewing in there," she said.

"What do you mean, we don't want him? Do you know who he is?" I asked.

"I don't have the slightest idea who he is, but I know we don't want him," she continued.

"He's one of the brightest Old Testament scholars in the world," I observed. "He's done enough research to fill a library. He's written a shelf full of books. He's a leader in the scholarly guild. He lived in Jerusalem for eight years. He's been teaching for more than twenty years. He's one of the best there is."

"We don't want him," she said.

"Why not?" I asked.

"Because when he talks, he looks right past you. He doesn't care a thing about you unless you have something he wants. He's self-centered and distant. There's nothing engaging about him at all. We don't want him."

Her words were prophecy: despite this man's enormous qualifications, he was not offered the job. The primary reason was otherwise, but I had to wonder if the "be nice" factor didn't play a role.

The main result of this "be nice" phenomenon is that it can be very difficult to know whether the person speaking to you is telling you the truth. In the name of being nice, a person may say one thing to you and be thinking exactly the opposite. You have to be perceptive to pick up the true communication, reading eyes, body language, innuendo. It is a treacherous game. You can be right in your reading or you can be entirely wrong, and you may never know which. I have seen people say one thing in one hour and exactly the opposite the next. It isn't dishonesty. It's the Louisville preference for being nice. It is important here to have mastered the art of not offending.

Those who come from the outside offer the greatest variety of evaluations of this phenomenon. I once heard a man from St. Louis blast it as the most undaunted hypocrisy he had ever seen, a shield of insincerity over everyone's true opinions, a cover thinly veiling raw exploitation by scheming combatants.

I also listened one evening as a neighbor who is not from the South described how she appreciates Louisville's surface of civility, suggesting that, far from perpetrating sham, it works to create the humaneness it conveys.

Whatever the evaluation, the "be nice" factor places a characteristically southern mark on Louisville.

And then there are the telltale marks. In Louisville almost any corner café will serve country ham and biscuits for breakfast. In Louisville you can still grow azaleas as long as you plant them close enough to the house that they can absorb some of its heat. In Louisville your neighbors will feel guilty if you move into a house and they don't visit you (and probably bring you food) in less than a week. In Louisville, if you have to be admitted to a hospital, your family goes with you, nearly camping out in your room. In Louisville a New York accent still sounds like it came from a different planet.

I recently asked two women who were joining my church to tell me the most noticeable characteristic they had found about Louisville. One woman had moved from Cleveland and the other from Boston. They each said the same thing. "The hardest thing to get used to here is the idea that I, a woman, am something men are supposed to take care of." That is southern.

Easily the most southern thing about Louisville is the Kentucky Derby. Here, on the first Saturday of May, the finest Thoroughbred horses in the world assemble under the twin spires of Churchill Downs for Louisville's two minutes of glory. Every blade of grass is brilliantly green and perfectly manicured. Every rose beams with colorful radiance. Every horse barn is freshly painted. Ladies don their elegantly styled dresses and flamboyant hats; men appoint themselves in colorful linen jackets, all according to the traditional graces of the southern plantation. The event occurs even when the temperature on Derby day is in the low thirties with snow flurries. Everyone sips mint juleps (although no one actually likes the wretched things, and, most certainly, no one drinks them at any other time of the year), and the ancient sport of kings and royalty is reenacted. In this moment, the entire world watches and takes Louisville seriously. It is easily the grandest day in the bluegrass year.

But it is far more than simply a horse race. It is the South reasserting its former glory, declaring that something grand and wonderful lived in these traditions. It is a day from the past restaged to awaken in us all the memory of the splendor that used to be.

Kentucky was deeply divided by the Civil War, with Louisville actually veering more Union than Confederate. But from the day the L&N Railroad pointed southward toward Nashville, Louisville has been at its heart and core southern.

Louisville is a crossroads city of about three hundred thousand people (nearly a million in the entire metropolitan area.) River, roads, and rails pass through it, and it has a major airport. It first became a settlement because the falls required boaters to come ashore as they moved up or down the Ohio River. The city was named in honor of Louis XVI for France's help to the colonies during the American Revolution.

The city has inherited a number of population groups. There is a large German Catholic population whose names remain very prominent in business and politics. There are eastern Kentucky immigrants who came when the coalfields were not doing well. The city is 19 percent African American, relatively low for the South because of the nineteenth-century Kentucky law limiting the number of slaves that could be brought into the state. There is an influential Jewish population that has established very strong institutions in the city. And now, more recently, there is a small but very resourceful refugee population from Korea, Vietnam, Romania, Cuba, Somalia, Bosnia, Iraq, and other recent world trouble spots. These people came to Louisville because of available employment.

A lot of people who live in Louisville consider it a really fine place and have no wish to move anywhere else. The pace of life is not hectic; Louisville is not growing at frantic speed. The green spaces are large and well maintained. The transportation system is quite negotiable. Arts opportunities in the city are characteristic of places many times Louisville's size. There is a major university and several well-regarded smaller colleges. The prevailing mood in the city is positive and optimistic. And, perhaps most of all, the city's life does not seem out of hand; the problems can still be solved.

My congregation in Louisville, Highland Presbyterian Church, is located just east of downtown in a well-preserved, century-old residential neighborhood. Many of the church's members are professionals: lawyers, judges, teachers, doctors, social workers, and businesspeople. The church also has an unusually high number of artists.

In a recent city election for mayor, both major candidates were members of Highland Church. (I kept totally quiet.)

The church's philosophy includes the belief that Christian faith should make us more open and tolerant rather than more rigid and narrow, more concerned with life in the present than life in the hereafter, more self-giving than self-serving. We have been very active in constructing low-income housing, in the resettlement of international refugees, in crossracial relationships, in Jewish-Presbyterian dialogue, and in antipoverty work.

The stories that follow come mostly from my relationships with church members.

I Can Handle it

It started when Adam was thirteen. He was at a party at a girl's house. Someone handed him a Coke. One sip made him realize it was more than Coke — bitter, strong. He was curious. He drank the whole thing. The kids laughed when he staggered across the floor and tripped on the carpet. They thought it was hilarious to see him sit down in a chair and miss. Someone had set him up. He liked it.

From then on Adam didn't think much about drinking. He just drank: a beer at a friend's house, a laced Mountain Dew at a school dance, a smuggled-in whiskey at a football game. He didn't crave it. He just liked it. It was just fun.

Two or three times he overdid it, found himself really out of control. His friends laughed. They told him he was hilarious when he was drunk. Adam couldn't see any harm it was doing. He went ahead.

College was a continuation—frat parties, football games. Adam's drinking became legal his junior year. No more fake IDs; no more asking friends to buy. He celebrated his twenty-first birthday by getting totally plastered, by far the worst he had ever done. His friends had to get him home and put him to bed. He didn't remember. He slept fourteen hours and woke up with a horrible headache that persisted for two days. He swore, "If this is where it leads, no more! I'm quitting!" He knew he didn't mean it.

Adam graduated from college and married Ellen, a girl he had dated for three years. Ellen knew that Adam drank, but she had never seen him really overdo it. Ellen got a job as a writer. Adam went to law school.

A week after he finished law school, Ellen had a baby boy. He was cute and captivating, just like she was. Adam took a job in the law department of a bank. Ellen scaled back her work but continued to write.

Then Ellen began to complain about Adam's drinking. "You come home at night," she said, "and sit there in front of that television sipping your drinks, and after a little while you're worth nothing—nothing as a father, nothing as a husband. If I say anything, you sneak upstairs where you have another bottle hidden. I know you work hard all day and need some letdown time, but so do I, and I need some help. Adam, you've got to quit drinking so much!"

Adam listened to this speech many times. He would reply, "I can handle it. I'll do more at night." His vow would last until the next day.

Ellen's complaints grew, not only about his drinking after work but about his behavior in social settings. It embarrassed her. She did not think he was funny. She was disgusted at having a half-drunk husband. Ellen objected frequently and strongly. Sometimes they argued. Adam stayed with his standard contention, "I can handle it." Ellen knew better. Their arguments continued.

Then their world turned upside down. Ellen was diagnosed with cancer. It was a strong, aggressive strain, not something easily stopped. She was young, vulnerable. The hospital would give her full therapy, do everything they could for her, try their best to beat it, but her situation was not good.

Soon thereafter, the family joined my church: Ellen in chemotherapy and fighting, Adam in alcohol and hiding, and their son, Joseph, now three, needing a firmer attachment to both Mom and Dad and not sure what was wrong.

Ellen fought valiantly but finally lost. I sat with Adam through her final morning and watched her die. It was beautiful—he was devoted to her—and it was deeply sad. We grieved together, cried, prayed, packed up her things, and left. Such times are painful, but they create enduring ties. I felt a bond. So did Adam.

After Ellen was gone, several friends shared Joseph's care while Adam tried to hold his work together.

One friend mentioned to me one day, "Does Adam drink too much?" Then another asked the same thing. I didn't see it, but I didn't see him very regularly. I wondered.

The tip-off came when I was visited by Joseph's preschool teacher, also a member of my church. "Adam is late picking up Joseph almost every day," she said. "I'll wait thirty minutes, an hour, sometimes two hours after school closes. I'll call his office. I'll call home. No one ever knows where he is. Then when he finally comes, he tells me he had to work late or that he had to get the car from the shop — some story I know isn't true.

"Yesterday Joseph and I were standing, gazing out the window together looking for Adam. He was forty minutes late. Joseph said, out of thin air, 'My Daddy had to work late.' It almost tore me up. Here was a three-year-old already learning to lie for his daddy, the family cover-up taking shape early. I know too many children who have shaped their lives around perpetrating that lie. They make up stories to help their parents save face. It's called codependency. That comment made me decide to talk to you."

I phoned several of Adam's friends, three in his business. I got the same message from all three: "Yes, Adam drinks too much. He tries to cover it, but it's transparent." One of them said the drinking had been going on for a long time.

Especially because Adam was a member of my church and a friend, I decided to go to a counselor to inquire about an intervention — a surprise meeting in which several friends confront the alcoholic with his alcohol use and bring as much pressure on him as they can to get treatment. We set up the intervention, how and when it would happen, who would be involved, and which alcoholic rehab program we would try to get Adam into. We worked it out with Adam's medical insurer. We even made arrangements for Joseph's care during the thirty-day rehab period.

This was on a Friday. The intervention was yet two weeks away. On Saturday afternoon, however, I had an premonition, a special feeling. I had become used to speaking very directly with Adam, pulling no punches, and I had the strange confidence that I could do it again. I knew that if I walked into his house and told him what had to happen, gave him no alternatives—just told him what he had to do, he would do it. He could get angry and throw me out. He could throw up his defenses and tell me I was crazy. But I somehow knew that none of that would happen. He would go. In retrospect, I don't think I should try this approach very often, but it worked.

I rang Adam's doorbell. I sat down in his living room. I looked him squarely in the eye and said, "Adam, I want you to come with me right now. We are going to enroll you in an alcohol treatment center. The plans are made. The center is waiting for you. Everything is ready. You and I are going. Come on."

"You think I need that?" Adam asked, only partially incredulous. I knew from that moment that I had him.

"Yes, I think you need it. Your drinking is affecting too many people."

"I can handle my drinking. I can stop any time I want." I had received the standard reply.

"No, you can't, Adam. Joseph's preschool teacher came by this week. She's worried about Joseph. She sees him making up stories to cover for his father—why you're late so much. Helping support his father's lie. He's trying to be your parent, Adam, because he knows something is wrong with you. That's a god-awful way to grow up, Adam, lying for your daddy. Joseph's too valuable for that. I'm not willing to let him go on."

I paused to see if I would get a fist in the teeth. No. I pressed forward.

"I called some of your friends. Adrian Smith said you smell like alcohol most of the time. Esther Gaddy said you've missed several business appointments for no good reason. Eric Doss told me that as your supervisor at the bank, he knows you drink too much and that if you don't stop you are going to lose your job. He says you're a good lawyer but that he can't count on either your mind or your body. And there are other people, Adam. I want you to go with me, right now, to the treatment center so we can enroll you."

"Right now?" he said. "Does it have to be right now?"

"Right now is the only time you will go, Adam. You won't go tomorrow. By then, you'll think of some reason not to. Right now is the only time. Get your coat."

"What about Joseph? He's over at Ginny Sorrell's house playing with their kids."

"I'll call Ginny from the center. She knows about this, and she'll be glad to keep Joseph for a couple more hours."

"Ginny Sorrell knows what we're talking about right now?"

"Lots of your friends know, Adam. We've talked about you a lot."

"Oh, God!" Adam lamented. "It's like having everyone looking through your front window."

"Eddie and Joyce Murrow know, too. They are so concerned that they are willing to take Joseph for a month. He loves them and their kids."

"Eddie and Joyce Murrow know? Oh, damn!"

"The only thing they don't know is when Joseph is coming. Otherwise, it's all set up," I said.

"You've done a whole job on me. What if I refuse?" Adam said.

Feeling slightly less certain than before, sensing that I might be losing instead of gaining, I said, "You're not going to refuse, Adam. YOU ARE GOING. The only question is how long we need to sit here and talk about it." I wondered if he would pick up my uncertainty.

"Well, I guess it can't hurt to go talk to them," Adam said. I knew I had won. We drove to the rehab center.

In less than two hours, all the final arrangements had been made. Adam would spend the rest of the weekend with Joseph and then enter the twenty-eight-day live-in alcoholic rehab program on Monday morning. I was uneasy with the delay, doubting that the treatment center would ever see him again. But the intake nurse didn't seem concerned. I decided to trust her judgment.

I would learn later that as he walked out the door that afternoon, Adam was saying to himself, "This place will never hold me. I'll give it three days at most. Then I'm gone. It's a bunch of hokey shrinks who think they know what I need. I can take care of myself." Alcoholics have a relentless, unending way of lying to themselves.

Adam did report for treatment on Monday morning. He was put in a room with a forty-eight-year-old man who had been drinking for thirty-two years. The man was a physical wreck. His speech was slurred, his reactions were very slow, and his liver was almost gone — his whole body showed the years of abuse. Adam would say later, "I hated him at first. I almost turned around on the spot and walked out. If you hadn't been there, I probably would have.

"But then I started talking to him, and he was a good guy. I liked him. He was really pleasant and had a fun side.

"And then it dawned on me after about a day: this man is who I'll be in fifteen years. That's why they put me here. I could see myself living in that wretched body of his. I was terrorized! And I was even more terrorized when he told me that this was his fifth time through the rehab program, that it's really hard to quit. This was his last chance. Six more months on alcohol and he would be dead. He might die anyway."

Adam began with a conversation with the director of the counseling program, John, a very perceptive man who had been an alcoholic himself for sixteen years and knew all the lies. John just let Adam talk, tell his story, rationalize his behavior, describe how things really weren't all that bad. When Adam finished, John hauled forth his standard reply, "You don't really expect me to believe all that shit, do you? I know you're lying to me. I know you're lying to yourself. You can't control alcohol. It's got you by the throat. I've been where you are, and I can see that clearly. You're telling me exactly the same lies I used to tell myself. We're going to spend the next twenty-eight days getting you to believe what a liar you are, and then we'll try to do something about it."

Adam then entered intensive group-counseling sessions, three hours in the morning and three hours in the afternoon. After a week, the counselors emerged with the word that Adam was one of the hardest people they had ever tried to reclaim. He was too likable, too agreeable. He had built a solid wall of denial around himself with his agreeableness, and they couldn't get through the wall. He would sit in group meetings and say yes to everything, admitting his problem and confirming that he had to solve it, but then the counselors would realize that they hadn't really gotten through to him at all. His words were a sham. His chief defense against letting anyone get close was his agreeableness. The counselors were extremely frustrated.

In the second and third weeks, the counselors brought in the heavy artillery. Friends, business associates, family, me. We all looked Adam straight in the eye and told him as directly as we knew how how his drinking was affecting us and what the consequences would be if he continued. I talked about Joseph, how unwilling I was to let Joseph grow up telling lies for his father, and how unwilling I also was to arrive at an accident scene some night and find Joseph wrapped around a telephone pole because of his father's drinking. The barrage was relentless. It had to be painful. Adam made a tape recording of each conversation and replayed them for himself many times.

When Adam's twenty-eight days were over, no one had any idea whether we had accomplished anything. Adam had an entirely different attitude—on top of the world, awed by his experience, ready to recommend it to everyone. But no one could be certain. Had he genuinely undergone a conversion, or was he still the big con man he had always been? Adam would tell me later, "Secretly I gave myself two weeks. I thought I'd be right back with the booze after that."

Adam has married again, to a very supportive woman who rides the waves with him and Joseph. He has had a couple of setbacks, bad ones, but most of the time Adam stays clean. He attends Alcoholics Anonymous regularly. No one knows what will happen next.

I am not a prohibitionist. I have downed a few sips of alcohol in my life, especially in places where the water was unsafe to drink. I have a good friend who is a home brewer, and I enjoy his descriptions of making and drinking it. I know a number of people who enjoy alcohol with no apparent problem.

In my pastoral experience, however, alcohol destroys more lives than any other phenomenon. It creates irrecoverable addicts, people who can struggle for years and not make it out. It is blindingly deceptive; it lets us believe we are in control until far beyond the point when we are not. It makes us irresponsible toward people for whom we are responsible. It makes us consummate liars, and it deftly turns those who love and support us into the same thing. It destroys our spouses, our children, our businesses, our friendships, our reputations. It works its cruelty across years, leaving a trail of ruin to the third or fourth generation. It turns what should be healthy human bodies into trash and rubble. In our society, I worry more about alcohol addiction than drug addiction. Alcohol, after all, is legal, advertised on television. I wish our society would deglamorize it.

Unbounded Spunk

As a part of regular pastoral visitation, I scheduled a visit with Beatrice in her home. Beatrice was a ninety-nine-year-old woman who showed the frailties of her age, although she was still remarkably strong and spry. She made her way around her house slowly and haltingly with a cane, her sturdy black shoes thumping against the wooden floor. She took care of herself in most ways but employed a helper to do cooking and housecleaning.

Beatrice had a very sharp mind and could converse on a large number of subjects. She came at you with a kind of bullheaded intensity that bordered on intimidation, expecting your opinions to be as strong and well founded as hers were. Now and then a very subtle sense of humor showed through, letting you know that she did not take herself nearly as seriously as you might have thought. We engaged in a straightforward, rock-ribbed conversation that I enjoyed.

After thirty minutes, I commented on the baby grand piano in her living room. The top was propped open and sheet music was on the stand. "Do you play?" I asked.

"Every day," she responded. There was a resolution in her voice that seemed to convey special meaning, but she did not elaborate.

"Will you play for me?" I asked, curious to see what ninety-nine-year-old hands and fingers could do.

"Certainly," she replied, "I would be most happy to." She seated herself at the piano bench, engaged in a brief preparatory ritual and then broke into a Chopin melody. It was not perfect—there were glosses and missed notes—but she was remarkably good. I had certainly never heard anything like it from a ninety-nine-year-old before.

Several days later, I mentioned my visit with Beatrice to another church member. "Let me tell you her story!" the church member replied. I listened with great interest.

"A year ago Beatrice visited her doctor for her annual medical exam. In the course of the examination, the doctor commented, 'I really should have you doing regular exercises to keep your muscles and bones strong. But it would take some extensive learning on your part—you'd have to know how to do things correctly—and no one your age is going to learn anything new. I know better than to try.'

" 'No one your age is going to learn anything new' —
the words stuck in Beatrice's brain. She heard nothing
else through the rest of the exam. So offended was she that
she went home determined — absolutely determined —
that she would prove that that doctor was not only a
smart-aleck but that he was also wrong.

"When Beatrice was younger, she was a concert pianist.
Quite good! She played with symphony orchestras and
did a lot of individual concerts. She was widely known.
Now she is on a crusade. She has vowed to learn by heart
an entire Beethoven piano sonata and play it for her
doctor at her one hundredth birthday party. She prac-
tices and memorizes every day."

A year later that was exactly what happened. Beatrice
held her centennial celebration. The featured event was
a huge cake with one hundred candles arranged in the
shape of a piano. The featured guest was Beatrice's doctor.
She sat him in a chair and played the Beethoven sonata.
It was a performance she could justly be proud of. I imagine he was more careful what he said to her after that.

Annabelle was eighty-six when I first met her, living alone
in her apartment, perfectly able to take care of herself.
She had a quiet manner, not one to attract attention.
But she also was quite resolute, firm in her ideas of how
she was going to lead her life.

As I visited Annabelle, her story unfolded. She told it
very matter-of-factly, as if there were nothing strange or
unusual about it at all.

"Throughout my life, I wanted to see the Taj Mahal. I
saw a picture of it in *National Geographic* when I was a little girl, and ever since then I have had a consuming passion to visit the real thing. Don't ask me why. I have just
always imagined that it must be one of the most magnif-

icent structures anywhere. The pictures make it look majestic and beautiful. I have always wanted to see it.

"Throughout my life I never had the opportunity. I worked, got married, raised children, raised grandchildren, and never went. The right time just never came. I reached old age with this one piece of unfinished business.

"Five years ago I decided it was time. I was only eighty-one and had plenty of spark left. I got on the telephone and made all the arrangements. I would fly to New York, then to Berlin, then to New Delhi. I would take a train to Agra, visit the Taj, and return by the same route. It all seemed very simple: the last major thing I wanted to do in my life.

"I knew, however, that if my kids knew what I was doing, they would veto it. They would be too protective of me ever to let me go on a trip like that. So I didn't tell them anything until I was ready to leave Kennedy Airport. Literally an hour before departure, I called them from New York to tell them what I was doing. They were shocked! They were flabbergasted! They begged me not to do it, but I told them I was on my way. I wasn't calling to give them any choice in the matter.

"The trip went wonderfully. All my flight connections were perfect, and people along the way were very helpful. I had a lovely, wonderful visit to the Taj Mahal. It was everything I had expected. I could not have been more satisfied at having carried off the trip.

"Until I got back to New Delhi. Then I got sick, dreadfully sick. I felt awful. It must have been something I ate. I was really suffering in my hotel room until they finally took me to a hospital, an American hospital. By the time I got there, I felt like I was half gone.

"A young American doctor examined me. Told me I had a good case of dysentery. Scolded me for making a trip like that by myself. Told me I ought to take more careful care of myself. He sounded just like my children — that's exactly what they would have said if they had gotten the opportunity. He said it was going to take a lot of careful effort to get me well again and back home safely.

"At that point, I had heard enough. I said to him, straight out, 'Doctor, all my life I have had a consuming passion to see the Taj Mahal. I have now seen it and I am happy. I do not really care that much whether I get back home. Getting home safely was not the controlling idea in my mind as I planned this trip. If I die here in New Delhi, I give you permission to tie my body to a wooden raft and float me down the Ganges River into the Indian Ocean, where I shall be happy through the rest of eternity. Simply do me the favor of notifying my children back home of what I have said to you, and send them my fondest love.'"

As Annabelle sat alone in her condo, I could only wonder what the next chapter might be.

A Tale of Two Congregations

West Chestnut Street Baptist Church is located ten blocks west of downtown Louisville. It is a fourteen hundred–member African American congregation founded in 1886. It embodies a proud and distinguished history. Its pastors have included some of the city's most gifted, especially at preaching. It has raised numerous generations of young people, providing spiritual growth and guidance to hundreds of young lives. It has produced some of the finest black gospel music in the region, with children's choirs, young adult choirs, chancel choirs, and senior citizen choirs that can sing with the best.

In the 1950s, '60s, and '70s, West Chestnut played a key role in the struggle for civil rights in Louisville, serving as a training center for protesters. It welcomed a formidable list of civil rights leaders to its pulpit: Fred Shuttlesworth, C. T. Vivian, Andrew Young, Jesse Jackson, Martin Luther King Jr., and others. West Chestnut has stood among the giants in Louisville's West End.

Highland Presbyterian Church, my own congregation, is located about ten blocks east of downtown Louisville. Mostly white, it was founded in 1882. It bears its own distinguished history. The congregation includes more talented people than I can count, from judges, aldermen, business leaders, and teachers to artists, city planners, and musicians. It sponsors the longest continuously running radio show in Louisville, its worship sermons, which have been on the air for more than fifty years. For nearly forty years it has run a weekday preschool that now counts among its graduates some of Louisville's leading citizens. It houses the Kentucky Refugee Ministry, which resettles five hundred to six jundred international refugees each year into Kentucky. It is an activist church, strong in its commitment to urban life.

In 1983, during the era of "benign neglect" in race relations in this country, when we were doing our best to pretend that the race problem had gone away, Dr. C. Mackey Daniels, the pastor of West Chestnut, and I met over lunch in a downtown restaurant. Our purpose was to see if we could forge a relationship between our two congregations that would speak strongly to the city on behalf of racial unity. American society, we believed, could not afford to let its black and white communities drift into separated enclaves. Devoted effort — hard work — would be needed to bring these two quite different peoples into a functioning unity. Dr. Daniels and I both bore the conviction that this was the only way for the nation to travel.

C. Mackey Daniels was born in South Carolina at nearly the same time I was born in North Carolina. We were college students at universities just a few miles apart. We both were deeply moved by the preaching of the young Dr. Martin Luther King Jr., and we both experienced the enormous passion that swept the nation in the early years of the civil rights movement. We both bear the conviction that racial segregation is wrong and needs to be replaced by a living relationship. We both, in one way and another, have devoted our lives to that cause. Our backgrounds are remarkably similar, only he is black, and I am white.

For one notable reason, among others, I was delighted to be connecting with West Chestnut. The reason was that my congregation would find it nearly impossible to patronize them. Presbyterians have an unending tendency to patronize. We think of ourselves as educated, upper-middle-class people who know well how to deal with life, and we want, with perfectly good intention, to help those not as far along as we. West Chestnut did not need to be helped in any way whatsoever. They were bigger than we were, stronger than we were, with a music program larger than ours and a history easily as distinguished as ours. And their preaching was in a class by itself. Our relationship would involve two equals sharing their strengths, not two unequals trying to act as if they were equal. I was glad that, from the start, there was no cause for patronization.

I once heard Anne Braden, a white civil rights activist in Louisville since the 1950s, say from deep in her heart, "I discovered that the most profound racial prejudice in me is my presumption that blacks need my help, that I should show up so they will know how to do things better. They don't need me at all! They can run their movement perfectly well by themselves. They are simply nice enough to let me tag along and add something small here and there."

The relationship between the two churches has been the conjunction of two different cultures. Our worship styles differ. Our music differs. Our senses about formality and informality differ. Our histories differ. The ways we see and judge situations often differ. Our ways of making things work well differ. But all these differences have been transcended by our mutual determination to make the relationship work. We have learned a lot of compromise, and we have also learned how, very beneficially, to be changed by each other. The overall outcome, in the words of West Chestnut member Judy Kelly, has been that "Now we all feel like family."

C. Mackey and I determined that we would begin the relationship with a worship exchange. On a designated Sunday, he and his choir would come to Highland to lead our worship, and I and my choir would go to West Chestnut to lead its worship. Our shared worship experiences, once each year, have been the backbone of the relationship.

I remember vividly the first time I preached at West Chestnut. The worship service began at 11:00 A.M. There were four hymns, three anthems by the choir, five prayers, two announcement periods, a time of fellowship and friendship, two Bible readings, and three offerings. No one was in any hurry. My sermon commenced at 12:25 P.M. I preached seventeen minutes. When the service ended before 1:00, several people commented on how short it had been.

The service was characterized by well-organized formality. Several dozen people — deacons, ushers, stewards, readers — knew exactly how to carry out their roles in a highly ritualized way. And yet there was also an underlying informality. People in the congregation would move freely from place to place to greet one another or to carry out a duty. The overall design was meant to acknowledge that we were gathered in the presence of God — a strong sense of awe ran throughout — but also to say that we were good friends and that worship was a place to tend those friendships.

West Chestnut had a wonderful organist who provided a musical undercurrent for nearly everything. Whenever she felt moved, whenever she felt she wanted to intensify the spirit — during a prayer, an announcement, or the sermon — she would come in beneath the proceeding with a low, soulful melody. People would sway with her as she bore us along. She was obviously experienced. A lesser talent would have sounded completely out of place, but her timing was impeccable. Hers was surely one of the greatest talents in the room that day.

As sermon time approached, I felt I was about to stand on holy ground. I knew that the civil rights movement, with its ranks of courageous marchers devoted to nonviolent persistence, had been born and nurtured in places just such as this, and I felt humbled as I prepared to stand in the space. I wondered what those who had stood there before me had felt — their fears, their anger, their determination, their drive. A wave of self-doubt swept across me as I compared what I was about to say with what I knew they had said. I almost felt limp. It helped me enormously, however, when the presiding pastor, a West Chestnut associate, prayed an earnest and heartfelt prayer asking that my words be co-opted by God in speaking powerfully to the congregation. Perhaps they were not going to compare me with Jesse Jackson; maybe I had a chance.

I had never before preached to "Amen!" and "Oh yes!" and "All right!" I knew it was coming, but the first experience was still total shock. I found myself pausing to listen, wondering if I were doing this correctly, breaking my pace. I felt clearly out of sync. But the congregation seemed to understand. They bore with me. And after a bit, their expressions grew to be very, very nice. The chorus of response made me feel that they were listening intently, that my words were meaningful to them. I soon found myself anticipating the next outpouring. After a bit, they had lifted me onto an oral carpet of support, and they were carrying me along. The sermon was no longer a monologue but a mutual creation. It was easy to see why the black church has brought forth generations of powerful preachers; the experience breeds strength. I loved it, and I still love it every time I preach at West Chestnut.

Reports from my own sanctuary were that C. Mackey and his choir set the place on fire, that the music had even Highland Presbyterians bouncing in their seats and that the preaching reverberated from every wall. C. Mackey preached a memorable sermon, challenging the congregation to a new racial harmony. At one point he turned to his choir and exhorted, "You're going to have to teach these Presbyterians how to listen to a sermon!" at which moment they showered him with response. At another point he stopped dead still, looked up at the large chandelier that hangs in the middle of the sanctuary, and pleaded, "Chandelier, will you *please* shout, 'Amen'?" Several people agree now that it did. The hour consisted of a spirited band of Christians doing their best to teach a subdued band of Christians enthusiasm—which in Latin literally means "in-God-ism." Ever since that day, the "West Chestnut style" has been a factor in our worship thinking at Highland, even though we could never do it the same way they do.

Our most cherished worship experience occurred about nine years into the relationship. On Fourth Street in downtown Louisville there is a huge old show theater called the Palace. It has a gargantuan stage, two large tiers of padded seats, ornamental walls with statues on either side, and an indirectly lit blue ceiling with twinkling lights shining through tiny holes to simulate stars. Garrison Keillor, who performed there recently, said, "This place looks like it was designed by Baptists who were jealous of the Catholics."

Our two churches rented the Palace for a Sunday morning so that we could worship all together in one place — we had previously simply traded preachers and choirs. The worship, however, did not begin in the theater. It began on Broadway, several blocks distant. C. Mackey assembled his congregation at Seventh and Broadway, a few blocks toward downtown from his church, and I assembled mine at First and Broadway, a few blocks toward town from my church. At the appointed hour, a horn player at Fourth and Broadway sounded several enormous blasts on a shofar, a ram's horn used in ancient Hebrew tradition. We could only hope that the guests at the Brown Hotel, just across the street, were already awake. At the shofar blasts, the congregations began walking toward each other on Broadway, both singing, "In Christ There Is No East or West." We met at the Fourth Street intersection, symbolically stating our conviction that our two ends of town, one predominantly black and the other predominantly white, are called by God to meet and unify. There was a general time of greeting in the intersection when our people celebrated old friendships and created new ones. Youth from the congregations raised a huge banner that declared, "Highland Presbyterian and West Chestnut Street Baptist: Two Peoples, One Destiny." Following the banner, the congregations marched together two blocks on Fourth Street to the Palace.

Colorful banners from both churches overhung the stage. Both choirs assembled on risers. Pastors from both churches led the worship. We heard from Isaiah 19 about how God is building a highway to unite ancient antagonists. We heard that the hour is late, the time is short, and the task is urgent, that we must be about our Lord's business of creating unity. Children from both congregations assembled on stage to lead everyone in singing (and in some cases dancing to) the popularized tune, "A-men, A-men, A-men, Amen, Amen." Pastors and elders/ deacons from both churches served Communion. (This was the first time the West Chestnut congregation had ever received Communion from a woman, my pastor colleague, Elizabeth Kaznak Trexler.)

It was one of those glorious mornings when nothing could go wrong. Both congregations understood the point in what we were doing and felt 100 percent good about it. Diversity abounded, but it all unified in a single spirit. I wished I could have captured that moment and saved it forever.

No one seemed to notice that the entire proceeding lasted two hours and twenty-five minutes.

Each summer, our two churches sponsor the Court Education Project. Several members from West Chestnut join several members from Highland in the district courtrooms of the Hall of Justice. We sit in on felony/misdemeanor court, warrant court, and traffic court. We talk with prosecutors, defense attorneys, bailiffs, and judges. We tour the county jail. An orientation class initiates the project and a debriefing dinner ends it.

The courtrooms are a different world! Jammed with people, they are a revolving door of arrest, charge, negotiation, plea, and sentence. "Correction" (the jail is operated by the so-called Department of Corrections) appears to be a rare commodity. Many of the people who appear in court seem to view it as a game they try to win rather than as an opportunity to change their lives in any positive way. It is hard to tell who is less satisfied with the system: those put on trial by it or those who run it.

Our presence transforms the courtroom. The attorneys become more civil, the judges more respectful, the police officers more helpful. Everyone reflects the awareness of being watched. For this reason alone, it would be valuable to have those courtrooms stocked with outside observers at all times.

The main value of the Court Education Project occurs in the debriefing. Black people and white people can sit together in the same courtroom and see two entirely different things. (Indeed, black people and white people can walk together down the sidewalk and see two entirely different things.) The hidden prejudices, the implied put-downs, the lowered expectations, the patronizing moments, the subtle injustices: black people pick up on all of it. White people may well not pick up on any of it, because it is not aimed at us. As a number of writers have pointed out, to be black in America is an experience white people simply do not comprehend.

Many black people have grown up with a heavy skepticism toward how they will be treated by law-enforcement authorities, a skepticism most whites do not share. Black people expect that the police will more prone to bully them, that the court will more likely find them guilty, and that the judges will probably sentence them to stiffer penalties because they are black. That expectation comes as a revelation to white people. Increased comprehension of each other is, without question, the greatest accomplishment of the Court Education Project.

In a recent debriefing, the group was pondering the futility of the courtroom scenes they had just witnessed. Most of it seemed like a colossal waste of time and a very inefficient use of public money, and the observers had finished their time in court feeling depressed. They began to ask what they might do to improve the situation. One or two folks expressed doubt that useful changes could ever happen. Then a young man from West Chestnut, Dewayne Hanes, made the most pertinent observation of all: "I'm a fireman. Thirty years ago, the main thing firemen did was put out fires. There were lots of them, and we would go racing here and there trying to put them out. Then it occurred to someone: there must be a better way. Today, the main thing firemen do is try to prevent fires. We circulate all over the city advising people on how to make their buildings safer. And there are a lot fewer fires now and a lot less damage. And we're all happier. Maybe the way to improve the courts is to improve life on the streets."

It was a beautiful analogy.

A friend and church member, Rob, is a pilot for United Parcel Service. Rob flies very large jet airplanes around the country, delivering cargo to a variety of cities such as Seattle, Dallas, and New York. His oft-used smile defines him; aside from his skills as a pilot, Rob is a good-hearted fellow who relates genuinely and warmly to people around him.

Highland Church and West Chestnut Street Church send about sixty-five adults once each week to J. B. Atkinson Elementary School in Louisville's far West End. For several years, Atkinson has ranked lowest in reading scores of all fifty-two elementary schools in the public system.

It is located in one of the city's high-poverty areas, albeit in a new and very nice building. Our sixty-five adults travel there to spend forty-five minutes or so reading with children, one on one. Many of the adults are businesspeople downtown who devote one lunch hour per week to the Atkinson Reading Program.

It is too early to tell yet whether this program will make any discernable difference in the school's overall reading scores, but that has become purely secondary. The children absolutely love having an adult who comes to read and interact with them, individually, once each week. And the adults become quickly addicted: who does not enjoy nestling in with a child over a good book? As one Highland member who writes for the *Louisville Courier-Journal* said, "That one hour at Atkinson each week places in perspective all the other hours I spend at the *Courier*." It is the best means I have ever seen for putting large numbers of upper-middle-class adults into direct and meaningful contact with people and events in a low-income neighborhood.

One day as I headed out to Atkinson to read with my young charge, a second-grader named James, Rob happened to be in the church office. I asked him if he had time to go along with me, because I was sure I could find him a child to read with. He decided he would come along.

We arrived at the school to find the entire first three grades absorbed in a magic show in the school auditorium. I spotted James and asked him if he would like to read or if he would rather stay for the show. He wanted to stay.

As I got up, however, a third-grader named Tomika was at my heels. I had met Tomika before. She was an animated, highly imaginative nine-year-old. She loved to interrelate with people. "Will you read with me?" Tomika inquired with a tinge of excitement. I realized that she had come all the way from the other side of the auditorium.

"I will certainly read with you, Tomika," I said. "But I also have Rob here with me, and he wants to read with someone. Can you find a friend who would rather read than watch the magic show?"

"Sure," Tomika said as she trailed off to her original location. In a moment, she came back with another third-grader, Angela, who showed the same excitement as Tomika.

"Are you sure you want to leave the magic show?" I asked them both.

"This magic show is weak!" whispered Tomika. "I've seen all his tricks before, and I know how to do half of them." We headed down the hall toward the school library.

Rob read with Angela and I read with Tomika for perhaps thirty minutes. Both girls were absorbed.

Then Tomika said, "Can we get together and just talk for a little bit? I love to just talk." The magic show assembly had not let out yet, so Rob and I agreed.

Tomika found in a trash can a cardboard tube from the middle of a roll of paper towels. She turned it into an imaginary microphone and held it to her mouth. "I'm going to show you how my preacher preaches," she said. With shouts and arm waving and body contortions, Tomika did a dance that mimicked her preacher. We were thoroughly entertained.

Then she stopped, looked me straight in the face, and said, "I'm going to call you Reverend Jim."

"Tomika," I asked, "how did you know that I am a preacher? I haven't told you that."

Tomika paused, gazed at me straight in the face, and said, "I knew it because I can see God in your eyes."

Rob melted right on the steps of the reading center. So did I. That comment fueled my engines for the next month. Big gifts sometimes come in small, unexpected packages.

American society continues to struggle with the question of whether it intends to separate into racial/ethnic enclaves or whether its purpose is to bring the diverse peoples of this land into unity. There are paramilitary groups, there are social organizations, there are churches devoted to separatism, and the ideology of separatism is disguised in many costumes. Will we become a nation divided, or can we find our way toward unity?

Highland and West Chestnut continue to proclaim what we believe: that unity is the only way, that the hard work of mutual understanding is our challenge, that one nation indivisible is our goal. We bear that banner into the future.

Secret Lives

Paula Fleming came across as a humble, uncomplicated little woman who made her way through life without attracting much attention. A widow in her late seventies, Mrs. Fleming lived in a modest four-room frame house in a somewhat rundown residential neighborhood. Her husband had worked his entire adult life for "the railroad" (which meant the L&N) "somewhere on the labor side," doing whatever they needed him to do. He had "passed" eighteen years earlier. Mrs. Fleming now lived alone, making do with very little. She had friends in her neighborhood and in our church who knew her and looked after her.

To pull in some extra cash, Mrs. Fleming sold trinkets and small gifts out of her living room. The entire front of her house was stacked with greeting cards, party favors, dolls, bracelet charms, necklace pendants, small toys, shelf decorations, and desktop novelties, all of which she had taken a liking to at a sale somewhere. I tried once to understand her selection principles, but they seemed not particularly profound: "I like red," or, "The little girls in this neighborhood wear a lot of lace." Her neighbors knew to come to her whenever they wanted to give a small gift or decorate a corner. Never did I visit that she did not send me away with several doodads that she thought my two young sons would like. Mrs. Fleming had lived in the same house for fifty years, and her "little business" had definitely become too big for its confines.

A message came to the church office one morning, "Mrs. Fleming is in the hospital. Someone broke into her house last night, raped her, and robbed her. She's badly beaten."

It was absolutely sickening to think about: this fragile little woman having absorbed a sexual assault and a pounding over what some evil monster thought he might find in her house. It was senseless, asinine. I traveled to the hospital feeling very heavy inside.

Mrs. Fleming was in intensive care, in no shape to be visited. She appeared to be held together by adhesive tape, and she was hooked to numerous tubes and monitors. I don't think she knew I had come.

A week later she had recovered enough for us to talk. "I was asleep," she recounted, "in the middle of the night. I was awakened by a loud crashing noise at my back door. It startled me out of bed. As I was turning on the light, this man came through my bedroom door. He saw me and came at me, clawing and swinging. The last thing I remember was when he hit me on the side of the head; it felt like a boulder. I don't remember anything after that.

"But I did get a good look at him. He was big, husky, young, maybe twenty-five. The most distinctive thing about him was his curly white hair. You noticed it immediately. It was not the kind of thing you often see on a young man. And he was powerful—there was nothing at all I could do against him.

"The police tell me he didn't steal much," Mrs. Fleming went on. "He ransacked several boxes in my front room but mostly just scattered stuff across the floor. I don't know why he had to beat me up. I would have given him everything there."

She was hurt, but she was also strangely calm. At this moment when she could have filled herself with rage against her attacker, she seemed to have no impulse to do so. I wondered why. Perhaps she knew about rage, that it could be even more destructive to her than the beating she had taken. I have seen that happen: people who, over time, recover from an event but do not recover from their own reaction. Rage can continue for years, tormenting every other relationship. Maybe Mrs. Fleming had seen it too and was determined not to do it. Or perhaps rage simply was not part of her nature. Despite her antagonism toward this man, she was not going to focus her life on him. To do that would have created a brutality far more profound. For whatever reason, after Mrs. Fleming had finished telling her story, she moved on to more pleasant subjects. I respected her.

After six more days, Mrs. Fleming went home. She was recovering well.

Five weeks later, it all happened again, only much worse. In the middle of the night, someone broke down the back door, raped her, beat her mercilessly—his time she had a broken hip and arms—and tore the house completely apart. There were emptied boxes, smashed lamps, shattered glass, pictures ripped from the wall, broken dishes, overturned chairs, spattered blood. The intruder must have been in a terrible rage. But again, except for the emptied contents of her pocketbook, he didn't seem to have found much to steal. Mrs. Fleming was in poor condition back in the same hospital.

All over again it seemed grotesquely stupid. Who was this creep who seemed to need to rape and beat up old women in his search for thrills and for that night's cigarette money? The idea that he was roaming the neighborhood was chilling. People bolted their doors more tightly and installed security pins on their windows. They also kept a more vigilant eye out for one another.

Looking over Mrs. Fleming's house the next day, I realized that she would need a lot of help before she came back home — if, indeed, she ever did. Her friends could not let her return to this scene. I called two of our church members, Bill and Sally, to ask them to coordinate a cleanup.

Bill and Sally are as close to being angels as human beings get. Both retired, they now quietly spend their lives helping people. They have an uncanny knack for reading a situation, for figuring out quickly the right thing to do and say. On many occasions I have showed up in some need situation and found Bill and Sally already there. Their willingness to help knows no boundaries. They consider all members of the human family their brothers and sisters — from their close friends to newly arrived international refugees. And the most remarkable thing is that they refuse all recognition. They will smile graciously at a thank you, but they do not want any sort of public acknowledgment. Several years ago I nominated Bill and Sally for the prestigious Bell Award, given each year by a local radio station for exceptional volunteer service. They won! Out of probably fifty nominations, they won. They were to be featured in the newspaper and honored at a huge community banquet. But they turned it down. They didn't want the publicity. They simply wanted to continue to do their quiet, understated work in the lives of people in need. Every church should have a dozen Bills and Sallys.

Bill and Sally said they would gladly do what they could to help Mrs. Fleming. They arrived at her house the next morning to begin the cleanup.

Late the next morning, Bill walked into my office looking about twenty-five pounds overweight, bulging around the midsection. He had a very strange look on his face. "Guess what!" he said, his eyes twinkling.

"What?" I replied.

"Little Mrs. Fleming has a side to her none of us ever knew. We found shoe boxes — lots of shoe boxes — stacked on shelves in her basement. We didn't fool with them at first, thinking they were probably full of her old shoes. But finally we decided to open one. Look what was inside!" He began emptying his pockets onto my desk: stack after stack of ten- and twenty-dollar bills, a huge pile. I couldn't believe what I was seeing; the mound grew bigger. "That little woman must have cashed all her husband's pension checks for eighteen years and stored the money in her basement," Bill said. The money kept coming. I was incredulous. Finally, he stopped. "That's not nearly all of it, but that's all I could carry this trip. I'm on my way to the bank. I found some deposit slips in her desk, which means she must have a bank account, even though it doesn't appear she ever used it." We loaded Mrs. Fleming's money into a brown grocery bag, and Bill left.

What could Mrs. Fleming have been thinking? Did living atop all that cash make her feel safe and secure? Did she find some inner comfort at having it all nearby? Or did she not trust banks? Did she think they would someday fail as they had during the Great Depression? More than a few people who lived through that time lacked faith in banks. Or was she saving the money to give to someone, some cherished relative or friend? As far as we knew, she had no living family. Or had she just stashed it away little by little without thinking about it that much? Who knew her mind?

The secret lives some people nurture are beyond the imagination. I have related to some people for two years, five years, ten years, walking the path and thinking I have come to know them pretty well. But I haven't. There emerges some huge area that was invisible, a completely hidden facet. Out of all her friends, no one had known this side of Mrs. Fleming. I should stop being amazed.

And then there was the burglar—the irony of his thrashing about her house and missing completely the huge abundance of the very thing he was looking for. It was just barely beyond his reach. Almost comic! How could he have been so close and missed by so much?

The next day Bill showed up with more money. He and Sally were still uncovering shoe boxes.

And the next day, more; now they had found shoe boxes on the closet shelves. The treasure hunt continued for four days.

When they thought they had uncovered everything, a friend of theirs dropped by to witness their cleanup project. The friend looked at the desk in Mrs. Fleming's front room and asked, "Have you checked the secret compartment?"

"What secret compartment?"

"I have a desk exactly like that," the friend said. They opened the secret compartment, and out fell fifteen hundred dollars.

When Bill and Sally finally believed they had found everything, the total cash count was just over sixty-three thousand dollars. We felt a little uneasy about how Mrs. Fleming might feel about having it in a bank — she obviously had not wanted to put it there herself — but putting it in the bank seemed better than leaving it in her untended house.

After three weeks, Mrs. Fleming died, still in the hospital. This second trauma had proven too much. Neighbors and friends mourned her death. We gathered to speak our farewell words and to thank God for what her life had meant to us. It was a nice ceremony, attended by perhaps thirty people.

Word around the funeral was that the police were searching even harder for the burglar now that the charge included murder. They had gone door to door through the neighborhood, asking if anyone had seen or knew anything. The police were talking to a lot of people. We hoped they would succeed.

Bill and Sally had found Mrs. Fleming's family record. She had one great-niece who lived in Pittsburgh. The great-niece remembered Mrs. Fleming, but they had not communicated in years. The great-niece was a very nice woman who came and mourned with us. The money would go to her.

Three months after the funeral, the police made an arrest, a young man who lived about five blocks from Mrs. Fleming. Across the neighborhood he was regarded as absolutely no good, a bully who had never done anything but feed his own appetites. The neighborhood was not surprised at his arrest.

The man's own father had turned him in. Hearing the story of what had happened to Mrs. Fleming, and putting two and two together, the father had realized his son was the culprit. This fact added an even more pitiful note to an already sad story.

I decided to visit the suspect in jail. I made the appointment and presented myself at the Jefferson County Detention Center. The jail official ushered me into a very bleak, sterile room where thickly wired glass separated me from the prisoner side. I sat waiting. The door opened, and in walked a big, husky young man, perhaps twenty-five. The first thing I noticed was his curly, white hair— very unusual. I felt a tinge of satisfaction, fairly certain that they had arrested the right person.

Our conversation was stilted. Not only did we come from two different cultures, but he needed to keep up the pretense that he knew nothing at all about Mrs. Fleming. I was not there to raise the question of whether he was guilty, only to discover who he was and to hear anything he wanted to say about his situation. He asked at one point about Mrs. Fleming, "Who was she? I don't know nothing about her." We played the game for twenty minutes. He didn't seem to mind that I was there, but he also didn't seem to place any particular significance in my presence. We were simply two strangers talking. His greatest concern was where he would find his next pack of cigarettes; he had run out the night before. He carefully maintained his own secret life.

At his trial, the state presented telltale evidence, a few trinkets found at his home that matched items in Mrs. Fleming's "store." He was awfully stupid to have kept those things, I thought. Either he wasn't very bright, or he really didn't care that much what happened to him. He seemed to live in a kind of "so-what?" resignation.

The state also had one witness, a somewhat simple, naive looking young man who said he had been walking up Mrs. Fleming's back alley around 2:00 A.M., "headed home after hanging out for a while at the Pic-Pac." In an entirely innocent tone that reminded you of the little kid next door, he told of hearing a crashing noise and then seeing the defendant running out of Mrs. Fleming's house. The defendant had come through the back gate and passed under a streetlight, so that the witness got a good look. He guessed that the defendant had not seen him. This young man readily identified the defendant's curly white hair and had picked him out of a lineup.

Only in the hallway outside did I learn that this witness himself was in jail. He had three previous felony convictions ranging from fraud—stealing from an elderly couple—to auto theft. He was bargaining with the state to try to avoid a "persistent-felon" classification—a real jewel of a character. The defense contended that his testimony should be disqualified. Under Kentucky law, however, the judge ruled that his testimony was admissible and that his criminal situation was not to be discussed with the jury.

Based on this man's statement, the defendant was convicted and sent to prison for a very long time. I hoped, quite frankly, that they were not in the same jail.

How is it that in this creation the wheat and the weeds are thoroughly intertwined? How do great cruelty and great kindness occur in the same place? How do ugliness and beauty flow from one event?

The world and its Creator will only let us cry for so long. After that a light shines to suggest that there is an empty tomb. It is one of the great, unforeseen graces I experience repeatedly in life.

Wireless Transmission

I had recruited Charlie Plummer to lead the Prayers of the People in worship one Sunday morning. Charlie was very thoughtful and articulate, a man of considerable spiritual devotion, and I looked forward to hearing what he would pray. I knew it would be well done.

Charlie, unlike others before him, wasn't going to have to come to the front to speak through the pulpit microphone. We had recently purchased a new sanctuary sound system, and the system included a wireless mike. All I had to do was attach a small transmitter, about the size of a cigarette pack, to Charlie's belt and the tiny clip-on mike to his lapel. He could simply stand at the pew where he was sitting and lead the prayer. The wireless pickup was effective from anywhere in the church building and probably outside for a quarter block. After years of dragging a trailing wire, I had found this little gadget a huge boon.

Charlie tried it out before worship. He sounded great: very clear, distinct, and easy to hear. His voice enveloped the sanctuary. I showed him how to manipulate the tiny off-on switch on top of the transmitter. When all was ready, I left Charlie and went to my office to complete my own preparations.

About eight minutes before worship began, Charlie decided to slip out to the rest room. Some people, even though they are accustomed to speaking in public, find church worship different. Charlie was one of them.

Entering the rest room and approaching a urinal, Charlie made his preparations. He didn't realize that as he negotiated his trousers, he turned on the tiny transmitter—it took only the slightest nudge. No warning light flashed; no sound came from the transmitter. Charlie knew not.

The microphone worked perfectly. The entire congregation listened to the characteristic noises of Charlie's urinal negotiations plus his conversation with the man at the next stall. The congregation sat at first in stunned silence; then they understood.

By the time Charlie got back, the whole place was breaking up. People shot sideways glances, but no one could look him in the face and tell him.

Charlie led the prayer. It was beautiful. I hope to get others to do half as well. The congregation would have been moved, except that no one heard a word. Their minds were somewhere else. Poor Charlie!

Everything's Going to Be All Right!

I had just climbed out of my car in downtown Louisville and was headed toward the front entrance of the public library. Ascending the library's stone steps, I heard a very loud metallic crash. I looked left and realized it had come from the intersection of Fourth and York Streets, a quarter block away. Two cars had arrived in the intersection at the same time at a ninety-degree angle. I wasn't sure which had run the red light. They had collided hard. The damage was not immense — they had not been traveling very fast — but a front corner of each car was flattened. Neither vehicle would go anywhere without a wrecker.

After a few moments, the drivers of both cars opened their doors. Each stepped out. One was a black woman, tall, stately, erect, in her late thirties, wearing a fairly dressy dress that told me she had probably been to a professional seminar or a luncheon of some kind. She still had a name tag and a flower on her lapel.

The other driver was a white woman, shorter, older, more stooped, dressed more casually. She looked as if she might live in a downtown condo and be on her way to the grocery store. She moved less resolutely.

For an uncertain moment the two of them paused, looking at each other, neither quite sure what to do next. I don't think I really expected either one to pull a gun and start shooting, but I did expect words to fly. They were shaken and upset, and I thought their distress would pour out across the intersection.

After a moment, they advanced toward each other, very tentatively, each trying to read the other. Then, as if some silent utterance spoke the same message to both of them, they hugged, an enormous, heartfelt embrace. It was an activity to which both were obviously accustomed. They stood there for several moments, patting each other on the back, sharing their relief.

"I am so sorry I have messed up your new car," the white woman said, "I never once saw that stoplight." Her lawyer would have had a fit.

"You haven't done anything the garage can't fix," the black woman said. "It's not new, anyway. I've had it four years, and it's getting old."

"Are you okay?" asked the black woman. "I was afraid you had hit your head on the windshield."

"I'm fine," said the white woman, "I didn't hit anything. Are you hurt?"

"Not at all," said the black woman, her arm still draped around the shorter woman's shoulder. They consoled each other for several more moments.

I had moved quickly toward the intersection to see if either of them needed help. Now I paused, wondering: is there any way these two women could preserve this moment and share it with the world? Is there any way our adversarial, contentious society might learn basic human relatedness from these two experts?

The black woman was still comforting the white woman, "Don't worry, sweetheart, everything's going to be all right." Somehow I believed it was.

Faith Healing

A local television station called to ask if I would participate in a debate on their early evening "events in the city" program.

A church in Louisville was having a revival, an event designed to enliven the spirits of its current members and to interest new members. To lead the revival, the church was bringing in a well-known faith healer, a man they said had "cured thousands of people of their infirmities." I had never heard of him, but that did not belie their claim. The healer, they advertised, could fix any ailment: arthritis, heart disease, kidney problems, emphysema, even cancer. His prime act was to stand before a church congregation, pull out his eyeball, display it to the people, place it back in its socket, cover his opposite eye with a patch, and then read anything the congregation put in front of him. This little act had created his renown and attracted crowds to his appearances. It was clearly why the television station had decided to devote thirty minutes to covering his visit to Louisville.

The television station wanted to set up a debate on faith healing. The pastor of the revival church would represent one point of view; I was being asked to represent another point of view. Why they chose me, I have no idea. I had no attachment whatever to the field. Being a southerner, I had spent half my life in the vicinity of faith-healing tents and revival meetings, but I had paid little attention.

I also do not know why I consented to take part.

When I arrived at the television station, the revival pastor was already there, waiting in the lobby. We met for the first time. He seemed like a pleasant, congenial fellow, not particularly sharp-edged or intolerant but fairly easygoing. I guessed that we would have an amiable conversation, even if we diverged sharply in our views.

The host introduced the subject and showed a video-tape of the faith healer's act. Sure enough, the man appeared to yank his left eyeball out of its socket. He held it for everyone to see. It was hard to distinguish on videotape, but the object indeed looked like an eye. After everyone had had time to gape, the faith healer popped it back in. He then covered his other eye with a large black patch and asked someone to offer him something to read. He read the name and address from a woman's driver's license and also her social security number. The congregation was awed! They sat in rapt amazement, believing truly that what they were seeing was a miracle. The host then stopped the videotape, and our conversation began.

The revival pastor told of how many people this man had healed across the world — hundreds, thousands — of every infirmity known to humanity. Throngs would testify to his effectiveness; great numbers could tell of their own cures.

This man was surely a man of God. God was with him every step. The grace of God surrounded him. The power of God worked through him. Seldom had God placed on this earth a man so filled with the Holy Spirit.

God has been healing faithful people for thousands of years. God cured a leper. God restored a man's withered hand. God gave sight to a blind man. God stopped a woman's flow of blood. God drove out the evil spirits from a man possessed. God raised a little girl from death. In Jesus Christ, God came to heal our diseases and cure our infirmities. This man is Christ's ambassador, an agent to continue Christ's healing in a needy and broken world.

The pastor invited everyone to come to his church the next night to see for themselves. "You will believe it when you see it in person!" he said. "Your eyes will not lie to you. Come tomorrow night and join us in this profound experience of faith!"

The host turned to me for my reply. "If a person has been healed," I began, "I rejoice! God can heal anyone God decides to heal. God healed people through Jesus Christ. God heals people now. I know people God has healed. I have watched it happen. It is a marvel, a wonder, a great gift! I believe in praying for God to heal us. I rejoice when God does!

"I strongly doubt, however, that any human being should advertise himself as one able to call down God's healing power. The God I meet in the Bible is not subject to human control, not ordered by earthly command. God does what God pleases, when God pleases, with whom God pleases. Faith is not a matter of God's conforming to what we want but of our conforming to what God wants. I think this faith healing is voodoo: you pray the right prayers, perform the right incantations, and God will bless you.

"There was a time in the New Testament when the Church was tempted to turn Christian faith into miracle religion. 'If you believe strongly enough, Jesus will heal you, just as he healed others!' said a number of New Testament preachers. 'If you have enough faith, Jesus will save you from difficulty, just as he saved others.'

"The writer of the Gospel of Mark rejects this. 'Faith does not mean being able to call down a miracle from God to heal us,' he says. 'Faith means enduring to the end as Christ's disciples, whether a miracle heals us or not.' I believe that God can and does heal people. But I do not believe in Christian faith as a miracle religion."

The host returned to the revival pastor. "Oh, well, our faith does not depend on miracles. We believe in Jesus

Christ whether they happen or not. And we're not calling down God's miracles. God certainly performs a miracle only when God decides to. We can't command it. But we can pray for it! We can ask for it! God says in the Scriptures, 'Ask, and it will be given. Seek, and you shall find.' We believe in asking."

I replied, "From what I saw on that video, it looks to me like you are guaranteeing a miracle. What else is taking your eye out and putting it back in?"

Our conversation went back and forth for the half hour. It was direct, but it was never bitter. We actually had a pretty good time presenting two sides. I thought the program went well.

Who won the debate? Whose side prevailed? That was not decided until minutes after the show was over. The revival pastor and I left the studio together and walked up the hall in conversation. We lingered in the station lobby as the host thanked us for what he said was a good thirty minutes. Then we walked together out of the building and into the parking lot.

Finally saying goodbye, the revival pastor got into a sparkling new Chrysler Imperial, and I got into a fourteen-year-old red Volkswagen Beetle.

Faith healing works! It works marvels, wonders! I have never doubted its power since that time.

Addicted

Every once in a while, I like to ease by the twenty-fifth floor of the Citizens Plaza Building in downtown Louisville. The twenty-fifth floor is elegantly appointed with deep reddish brown–stained woodwork, beautiful thick-pile carpets, glistening conference tables, well-selected art, and a general air of dignity. I like to go there to see my friend Grover, down the hall to the left in his corner office with the wide, panoramic view of the Ohio River. Grover is always dressed in a very nice business suit, often with pinstripes, because he is one of the senior partners of the distinguished law firm of Wyatt, Tarrant, and Combs.

I like to see Grover there because I know I will also see him at the Presbyterian Community Center, a neighborhood activity center in one of the most run-down, poverty-stricken areas of Louisville, Smoketown. I will see him there talking to an elderly resident of the Sheppard Square Housing Project, or joshing with a neighborhood ten-year-old, or leading a Presbyterian Community Center Board of Directors' meeting, or raising four million dollars to rebuild the center. Both that beautiful office on the twenty-fifth floor and that run-down building in Smoketown are places Grover knows intimately. He divides his life between these two callings. I have great regard for people who arrange themselves that way.

The Presbyterian Community Center is a hundred years old. It was established by students at Louisville Presbyterian Theological Seminary as a recreation and Bible study program for neighborhood children. Through the twentieth century, it has grown to include day care, recreational activities for young children and youth (basketball, football, baseball, boxing, and so forth), an older-adult activity program, music and drama organizations, and more.

Contiguous with the center on two sides is the Sheppard Square Housing Project, home to more than three hundred low-income families. The center is currently housed in an old, run-down building that was once a factory.

It has produced, over the years, more than its share of notable people, the best known being Muhammad Ali.

Grover was born in south Louisville, the only child of a milkman and a sales clerk at McCrory's five-and-ten-cent store. He attended the University of Louisville and subsequently graduated from the university's law school.

After serving in the U.S. Air Force, Grover joined the Louisville law firm of Wyatt, Tarrant, and Combs. His eyes were fixed on success, and the major vision he had at that point was personal success. He had been gifted with a very able mind, and success came. In two decades of work, he reached the top at Wyatt, Tarrant.

(The founding partners of the firm were Wilson Wyatt, who served as mayor of Louisville during World War II, chair of the National Housing Agency under President Harry Truman, and campaign manager for Democratic presidential nominee Adlai Stevenson; Kentucky Democratic Governor Bert Combs; and John Tarrant, a conservative Republican.)

Grover's community-service activities included commitments familiar to more than a few downtown businesspeople. He served as chair of the board of directors of the Louisville Boat Club (the most prestigious country club in the city). He was also chair of the the board of the private Louisville Collegiate School. He also served as president of the board of regents of Locust Grove, a historic home. And there were more.

Having grown up in a modest though very supportive south Louisville family, Grover had done exceedingly well. He was nearly the classic Horatio Alger, someone who by ingenuity, determination, and hard work had lifted himself from humble beginnings to extraordinary accomplishment. Grover rightly felt good about his achievements.

And then, the strangest thing happened. In the early 1990s, Grover took on new eyes. He began seeing things around him he had never seen before. They had been there all along, but he only now saw them.

There were several factors. One was that his best friend, Kenny, died suddenly of a heart attack at age forty-nine. It was a mournful, wrenching experience. In Grover's words, "Not only did I lose Kenny, but I also saw for the first time my own mortality." Another factor was Grover's participation in Leadership Louisville, a concentrated program designed to familiarize enrollees with large-perspective pictures of the city. A third factor was Grover's involvement in the Bingham Fellows Program, a Leadership Louisville follow-up designed to create commitment to some specific problem area in the city. Grover's Bingham Fellows class chose Smoketown, where the Presbyterian Community Center and Sheppard Square housing project are located, as their commitment.

Perhaps the biggest factor of all was that Grover married Gwynne, a very perceptive woman with an acute social conscience. Gwynne saw the world through different lenses, and her way of looking at things now entered Grover's life.

The pivotal event is well documented. Grover has told the story many times.

Grover had arranged for a local manufacturer to donate sheets of plexiglass to replace broken and cracked windows on one wall of the Presbyterian Community Center. He had dropped by the center after work one day to see how the installation was proceeding. On the sidewalk out front, he was greeted by the center's director, Edna McDonald. They stood and talked for several moments.

Four young boys came up to Ms. McDonald and said, "Miss Edna, we need some money to buy something to eat at the store. Will you give us some?"

She replied, "I won't give you money, but if you will go in the center and get some brooms and come out here and sweep clean this dirty sidewalk, I'll pay you for your work."

The boys agreed and disappeared inside the center. Reappearing with brooms, they went to work sweeping the sidewalk. As they were working, Grover reached into his pocket, pulled out four one-dollar bills, and handed them to Ms. McDonald, saying, "Here's the money you'll need."

Ms. McDonald replied, "Watch out, Grover, you might get yourself addicted!"

Grover replied, "I think I already have."

Driving home from the center, Grover found himself sobbing intensely. He had to stop the car once to wipe the tears from his eyes. He still does not fully comprehend what happened, but he realized for the first time that those four boys were his own children. They belonged to the same family he belongs to. Their future depended on him. It was profound, life changing, something like a flash of light on the Damascus Road. From that moment, Grover began rearranging his priorities.

I was working as the chairman of the start-up committee to raise the four million dollars to build a new Presbyterian Community Center. Grover joined that committee. When a permanent committee was established, Grover, with his considerable talents and his extensive knowledge of people across the city, became chair of the permanent committee. The campaign is now nearly complete under his leadership. Grover also accepted an invitation to join the center's board of directors. He is now its chair. He has made numerous visits to convince people and foundations that they should contribute to the center campaign. He has gotten to know every center staff member and no small number of neighborhood residents. He has examined alternative sites for the new center and participated in the selection. He has successfully negotiated with neighborhood residents to move their homes to other locations. He has served on the committee to choose an architect. He has done nearly everything. I expect to arrive at the center someday in the future and find Grover playing basketball with the kids.

This man has committed a considerable piece of his life to those four little boys and to the community they represent. They have ceased to be invisible to him; they are now high profile. And that is why I find considerable pleasure in dropping by the twenty-fifth floor of the Citizens Plaza Building — to remind myself of the other life from which Grover comes.

Samaritans

They had ten days of spring break into which to squeeze their vacation. David and Carl set off early Friday morning headed for a South Carolina beach. They would get the cottage ready and the food packed in. Their wives and the kids would come on Saturday.

The only trouble was that they would travel the first miles in a snowstorm. A late-winter blast had come out of the Gulf of Mexico, and a lot of snow was forecast for central Kentucky. It would be warm, wet snow, and it probably wouldn't last long. But the forecast said it would be big. With nothing on the ground yet, however, they left, nurturing the adolescent confidence that the storm would probably miss them entirely.

Forty miles east of Louisville, they were in snow. There was not much drop in speed, just in visibility. Suddenly, with little warning, they saw the traffic halted ahead. Cars had swerved right and left to avoid hitting one another. They managed to skid their van to a halt just in time. The eighteen-wheeler behind them didn't fare so well. It crashed into their rear, blasting them into a ditch. They were flattened both rear and front.

Carl, who had been driving, knocked his head against the steering wheel and was cut up pretty badly. David's ankle was crushed when the front of the vehicle compressed against his seat. Both of them suffered whiplash. They lay there several minutes in severe pain, trying first to ease themselves and then, slowly, to figure out what to do next.

Carl was able to work his way out of the driver's seat. He went back and tapped on the door of the truck cab. The truck driver seemed strangely unconcerned. He wasn't really interested in how badly they were hurt. He simply declared that there wasn't anything he could do and then snuggled up with his female companion inside his cab. It was weird.

From behind the truck, however, appeared a man and a women. They came forward to see what had happened. They were horrified, especially that the truck driver was doing nothing. They went into action.

From their van they called an ambulance from Lexington, nineteen miles away. The emergency service advised that it would do its best, but with the traffic tie-up, it would probably be hours before they could get there. "Try to devise some other way," they said.

At that point the man and woman began pulling wooden slats out of their van and assembling makeshift stretchers. When they got two stretchers made, they very carefully loaded David and Carl into the van. They used their coats as covers.

With the woman driving and the man playing nurse in the back, they began an incredible trek: along shoulders, between parked vehicles, down median strips, across ice-covered bridges, up long hills a few feet at the time, among downed utility wires. People along the route were helpful, but the nineteen miles still took three hours and fifteen minutes. All the while, the man kept vigilant watch, keeping them warm, binding their wounds, talking to them, encouraging them.

Finally they reached a hospital. By now David and Carl were hurting badly. The man and woman took David and Carl to the emergency room, checked them in, and filled out the paperwork. The man and woman phoned families back in Louisville, assuring them that despite the fairly serious injuries the two men would be okay. The couple delivered messages of encouragement back to David and Carl from their families. The two strangers parked themselves at the hospital through the night to make sure the two men were well cared for. In short, the man and woman treated two people they had never before met like members of their own family.

The next morning, the man and woman finally departed, knowing that the snowstorm had abated and that David and Carl's families would arrive by midday.

In three days, however, the man and woman were back, wanting to see how the men were. David and Carl tried to give them a reward for their remarkable service, a thank-you gift to show their appreciation. But the man and woman refused. Their reward, they said, was the grateful hearts of their new friends. They wanted no more.

Before they departed, David asked who they were, these two people who had poured out so much for their fellow human beings. The answer was a total surprise. She was a belly dancer, and he was a male stripper. They had come from St. Louis and been headed for a nightclub show in Charleston, West Virginia. They had missed their first engagement but had been able to make the final two.

As with the first Samaritan, civil society considered them degraded, uncouth. But Carl and David knew better.

A Lot of Small Stones

Abdul came off the plane with one duffel bag. It held everything he had brought from his former life. As I watched him, he looked understandably lost. He was a young man of twenty-six, black hair, slightly dark complexion, deeply set brown eyes, a bit quiet and deferential in manner but warmly engaging. He had arrived in a completely new culture amid people and customs he did not know. He had no idea what he would do after he got here or what sort of welcome he would receive. Everything was new. He spoke enough English to give him a touch of confidence, but he still bore the look of being fundamentally lost.

Abdul had come from southern Iraq. He had left there his entire family: sisters and brothers, mother and father. He had left his many friends. He had left there his accustomed way of life, his food, his routines, the town of Basra, which was his home. He was Shiite Muslim, a religion that many people in this country would find strange. He had been a civil engineer in Iraq, specializing in transportation structures. But, as with most refugees, his professional credentials did not transfer. He was essentially starting his life over.

At the beginning of the Persian Gulf war, Abdul and several thousand other young Shiites had identified what they thought was their moment of opportunity. They had rebelled against Saddam Hussein, ready to overthrow their longtime political adversary. They had prepared to support from within the country the United Nations initiative being waged from without.

But the coup had not happened. The war had ended with Saddam still in power. He had been weakened but not deposed. The young Shiites knew that Saddam would move swiftly against them. His police and military would quickly begin arrests. The Shiites would face prison and the usual fate of traitors — execution.

Thus Abdul and about twenty thousand other southern Iraqis — most of them young men — fled the country on foot. They crossed the southern border into Kuwait and then walked all the way across Kuwait into Saudi Arabia.

Saudi Arabia did not want twenty thousand Iraqi refugees. All, including Abdul, were herded into giant holding pens, enclosed compounds where they received enough food, shelter, clothing, and medical care to live until they could be relocated elsewhere. Abdul had lived in one of these compounds for two years before finally being processed and received as a refugee by the United States. Along with several friends, he arrived at Standiford Field in Louisville on a fall afternoon.

Abdul was brought here by the Kentucky Refugee Ministry, which operates out of my church. The ministry resettles about five hundred refugees each year across Kentucky. Abdul and eleven of his friends were placed under the direct sponsorship of my congregation, and various church members took up the task of relating to particular young men. My wife and I related to Abdul.

For a person who had been through all he had, I was amazed that Abdul was not more conflicted and angry. He told his story with great regret. He genuinely missed his family and home; he would much prefer still to be in Basra. But he was not wallowing in the loss. He knew that he had faced a choice—between becoming a refugee and being put to death—and he harbored no second thoughts over his decision. The day might come when he could return to Iraq, but he was not planning around that day. He was here to make the best he could of his new situation, and his major thoughts were to plan the steps in that strategy. He had what many arriving refugees have: a quiet determination to succeed.

I spent a couple of days with Abdul helping him get the lay of the land. We visited the local public library so that he could see what sorts of books were available to help him. We visited the University of Louisville and Jefferson Community College to inquire about courses and to see if any of his Iraqi credits might transfer. We talked to local engineers to see about engineering accreditation. We studied bus routes and schedules. We inquired about jobs to tide him over after his refugee stipend ran out in about two months. We visited food stores to discover where he might find things he liked. All together, the task seemed overwhelming. It was hard for me to see how Abdul would succeed. Enormous hurdles stood before him. But he was guided by a clear idea, which he articulated: "A lot of small stones will build a very large building," he said to me, a typical engineer's image. Abdul, I realized, had more faith than I did.

He remained a charming young man. His dark eyes glistened behind his black hair. I searched for cynicism but could barely find it. The "poor me" factor was even more absent; it was not in Abdul to pity himself. He seemed to expect that life would contain hard bumps, a lot of things that weren't fair, and he believed that his task was to surmount them.

A few weeks after Abdul arrived, Nancy and I invited him and three of his friends to Christmas Eve at our house.

It would be a halting evening—the other three spoke virtually no English at all—but we enjoy the challenge of making these sorts of things fun.

As we gathered, we learned that one of the men had telephoned his family in Iraq several days before. He had not talked long, just long enough to assure them that he was all right and to ask about them. It had been too long, however. A later phone call home by one of his friends had provided the distressing information that his younger brother had been arrested and jailed. The charge: talking to a traitor on the telephone. Our guest felt terrible, miserable, that he had put his little brother in jail, but he dared not call home again to express it. It was a bad moment.

Nancy had made careful dinner preparations. Knowing that Shiites do not eat meat, she had researched several vegetarian dishes she thought they might like. As we sat, she explained each dish. Abdul listened carefully and translated as best he could for the others. We have no idea what they heard. We do know, however, that for the next thirty minutes they acted like completely normal twenty-year-olds, taking a first helping, a second helping, and a third helping until the table was devoured. Whether it was their style or not, they seemed delighted at genuinely home-cooked food. The conversation remained slow, but the meal was splendid.

After dinner we played a very slow game of Scrabble. It took a few minutes for them to comprehend, but they did. We competed, taunted, and rejoiced in Arabic and in English.

Late in the evening, we took them back to their apartment complex, letting them out on the sidewalk. We thought Christmas Eve was over.

About eleven o'clock, the phone rang. It was Abdul. He was in the emergency room at University Hospital.

When he had walked into his apartment ninety minutes earlier, one of his apartment mates, Itti, had been inside with a knife. Itti, who tended to be volatile and get upset, had taken one look at Abdul and had slashed him across the face and body, leaving several nasty gashes. Abdul had managed to escape and call for help, but not before he had become a bloody mess.

Itti, virtually the opposite of Abdul, had had a very difficult struggle with their plight. From the walk across Kuwait through their stay in the Saudi holding pen to their arrival in the United States, Itti's dominant attitude had been that everything was wrong. He had been complaining, hard to get along with, depressed. On this night he had hit bottom. He had gotten a knife from the kitchen drawer and determined to vent his rage on the next person who came through the door. It had been Abdul.

Nancy and I went to the hospital immediately. Three or four slash marks traveled from Abdul's shoulder to his waist, and another divided his face. Itti had done a real job.

The police had arrested Itti and jailed him for assault. As Abdul lay in pain on the emergency room table, resembling a large, sewed-up rag doll, I could not believe my ears when I listened to what he said. "Itti is not a bad person. He is my friend. This has been a very hard time on him. He cannot be with his family. He has no good job. He is having a very hard time learning English. He is depressed about his home and his future. All of us could be like Itti. I do not want to take out any vengeance against him. I do not want to put Itti in prison. Let us just calm him down and go back to living the way we were. That's all we need to do."

There in that hospital bed lay a bruised, broken, bloody Shiite Muslim saying exactly the same thing a bruised, broken, and bloody Jesus had said two thousand years earlier: "Forgive them, for they know not what they do." I was sure on that Christmas Eve that I heard the voice of God.

Some weeks later I announced in worship one Sunday morning that Abdul and several other Iraqis were looking for jobs appropriate to their skills. I named their skills—a baker, a furniture maker, a mathematics teacher, a civil engineer—and asked if anyone in the congregation could provide leads. After worship a big, straightforward, plain-talking teddy bear of a man named Richard eased up to me and said, "Send me the civil engineer."

Richard runs a company that digs enormous holes for things like parking garages, hotels, and stadiums. The most delicate part of hole digging is formulating the bids, knowing what kind of ground has to be moved and calculating the cost. Richard intended to teach Abdul the skills of ground analysis, how to arrive accurately at dirt and rock volume, and so on.

Abdul, being a "project," went to work at a modest salary. Richard understood that it would be two or three years before Abdul would pay for himself. But he also quickly saw in Abdul a young man who would make it, an intelligent, self-motivated employee who would become an asset. Richard assured me repeatedly that the hiring had definitely been a good one.

Richard had a college-age daughter named Julie. Home on her summer break, Julie visited the plant one day and met Abdul. As she prepared to leave in the afternoon, she said to her father, "I want you to raise Abdul's salary."

"Why?" Richard inquired.

"Because I like him," Julie said.

"What kind of reason is that?" her father asked.

Julie said nothing.

The next pay period, Abdul had a fifty-cent "Julie raise."

Abdul advanced quickly. With Richard's help, he bought a car. Soon thereafter, he set up a car business on the side, purchasing good used vehicles, fixing them up, and reselling them. Richard also helped Abdul purchase a home. Abdul took engineering courses to improve his skills. Within a few years he had passed the engineer's licensing examination and became accredited. Shortly after that he became an American citizen.

One Sunday after worship, Richard approached me again. "What's going on with Abdul?" I inquired.

"That's what I came to tell you," Richard replied. "Have you been out to the new airport?" The airport authority had recently expanded its terminal building and built a large parking garage.

"Yes," I said. "It's nice."

"Did you walk through the tunnel that connects the terminal building to the parking garage?" he asked.

"Sure," I said.

"You may call that the Abdul Memorial Tunnel," Richard announced. "Abdul did that job."

"Amazing!" I said. "We've come a long way, haven't we?"

"A long way!" Richard replied.

I was proud. A lot of small stones will make a very large structure indeed!

I had to wonder what most of Louisville would think if they knew that their new airport tunnel had been designed by a Shiite Muslim Iraqi.

Keeping the Options Open

Every time I think I've seen everything, I learn I haven't.

My office phone rang in the middle of a workday. The female voice at the other end said, "Reverend, you don't know me. I am not a member of your church, but I drive by there every morning on the way to work. I have a question I need to discuss. Could I stop by this afternoon and see you? You might be able to help me."

"Sure," I said, and made the appointment.

She was in her late twenties, a lawyer, teacher, secretary, or something downtown — she didn't say what. Nicely dressed, well cared for, she looked like a typical middle-class young woman.

She didn't waste any time. "I have been living with a man for three years. His name is Steve. He's nice. I like him. He doesn't drink much and he isn't violent. We enjoy a lot of the same things. A good guy.

"Steve has asked me to marry him. He says he loves me and he'd like to make our relationship permanent. He says he'd like us to have our wedding this fall.

"Pastor, how do you know when it's time to get married? I don't have any idea. I've never lived around anyone who was married. My mother wasn't married when I was born. I have one sister in California who got married, but the marriage only lasted a few months, and I wasn't around her during that time. No one else around me has ever been married, and I don't know anything about it. How do you know when it's the right time? Is there any way to tell?"

The first thing I had to do was pick myself up off the floor. The question was not from my universe, and I had no ready response. I could have easily blasted this young woman with a moralistic homily on the seventh commandment, but that would have only answered my need, not hers.

I finally responded, "I would say that it's time for you to get married when you are genuinely ready to commit the rest of your life to another human being and to share with that other human being everything that happens to both of you. It's important that you find a man you will love and cherish. But it's even more important that you decide within yourself that you are ready to commit to someone for the rest of your life. That, to me, is the essence of marriage: a lifelong promise."

She thought about it for a moment and then said, "Well, there's one particular thing that really bothers me. I'm the fifth woman he's lived with, and I'm not sure I can trust him. He likes me now and things are fine. But what happens if he meets number six and wants to switch? Is he off and gone, and I'm left with nothing but a useless piece of paper? How can I be sure he won't do that? Is there some way for me to know if we are really ready to get married?"

She paused a moment, as if to let that part of her story sink in, which it slowly did. Then she continued. "But I have to admit that he's the third guy I have lived with, and I'm not sure he can trust me either. When you get tired of a man, it's definitely time to quit. No need dragging out a dreary relationship. Most men aren't very interesting that long anyway. I guess I like to keep my options open. Don't want to miss anything.

"Anyway, Reverend, can you give me any advice on what I ought to say to him. I do like him, but I have no idea how to tell whether it's time for me to get married."

I thought to myself, "The twenty-first century has just arrived in my office. Before my eyes sits a picture of where we are all headed if we keep going the way we're going now."

I restated that by my understanding marriage means lifelong commitment, not "keeping your options open." She seemed perplexed. It didn't fit her world any better than her question fitted mine.

Finally she said, "I want to discuss this with Steve and get back to you. He may want to come talk to you too."

"I would be delighted," I replied. "Please promise to come back and tell me what happens."

"I will," she said, "I promise." She left. I never heard from her again.

In her effort not to miss anything, this young woman was missing the most important thing of all: dependable, committed human relationship. I wished her growing up had given her a glimpse of that virtue.

I Could Be Your Son

I was profoundly affected. Shamsudin, Goran, Safet, Robert—strong, vigorous young men in their twenties, alert, obviously intelligent, joking, quipping, alive with conversation. And all with legs blown off.

"Why?" my heart cried out. "Why is it that these four young men, in the prime of youth, ready to dance with the world, would never again dance with anyone, their heavy wheelchairs a vivid reminder of the constraint that would follow them the rest of their lives? Why?"

They and six other Bosnian soldiers, all severely injured in the conflict with Serbia, had been flown into Louisville for medical treatment. Officially classified as refugees, they came under the sponsorship of the Kentucky Refugee Ministry. An entire one-floor section of University Hospital had been designated for their care. They would live there for several weeks—until rehabilitative surgery could be completed—and then they would move to nearby apartments for long-term recovery.

Their capacity to speak in English was limited to a few words they had learned from television and from tapes of the Police, apparently their favorite rock group. Our capacity to speak their language was nonexistent. Still, in the first days of their stay, their stories emerged.

Shamsudin was a powerfully built, barrel-chested young man with a gentle, good-humored approach to life—he loved dogs, cats and children. He had stepped on a land mine outside Sarajevo, blowing off both his legs. Friends and strangers had transported him 9/10 of a kilometer through an underground tunnel barely taller than a human being's chest to get him to the nearest hospital.

Goran was highly intelligent, a Bosnian chess champion with a voracious appetite for learning English. He had been in a trench when a grenade had blown off his right leg and seriously injured nerves in his left foot.

Safet, a police officer, had tried to take a bomb away from a man who had threatened to throw it into a crowded restaurant. The bomb had exploded and torn off Safet's left leg at the knee plus part of his right forearm.

And Robert, was a tall, lanky, soccer player who had not actually lost a leg but had come perilously close. Robert and several of his young friends in Sarajevo had organized a soccer game one afternoon in the name of keeping life in the city as normal as possible. His father had warned him, "Don't play soccer! Don't play soccer! The field is less than one kilometer behind the front line. It is too dangerous!" But Robert, sure as all twenty-two-year-olds are that nothing could possibly happen to him, slipped away and played anyway. A huge crowd had surrounded the field to watch the game—eight hundred people was Robert's guess. The game had grown so intense and noisy that it had become a target for the Serbs. Two grenades had hit the field almost simultaneously, killing sixteen people and injuring many more. Robert had been knocked unconscious, his left leg injured.

His friends, thinking he was dead, had called his father, who had come running, yelling "Robert! Robert! Wake up!" Robert had awakened. His father had scolded him, "Why did you play? I told you not to play! Look at you now! You are hurt!"

Robert had replied, "But Father, my team was ahead!"

That evening the Serbs had trained their loudspeakers across the city's dividing line and taunted, "Why don't you play another soccer game?" They knew what they had inflicted.

Robert's leg had been shattered. The bone was now infected. It would take two delicate operations and two years of recuperation in a steel-rod cast to restore his leg to its natural length.

A Bosnian who came to visit the four said to me, "The Bosnians, the Serbs, the Croats—they have all been neighbors, friends. They all speak the same language and bear the same lineage. Most of them got along fine before this insane war started. In ten years they will return to being neighbors, and no one will remember why they fought. But these and hundreds of other young men will be disfigured for life. It is all someone's lust for power, someone's craving to rule. It is lunacy, sheer lunacy—no one ever wins."

Over the next three weeks Shamsudin, Goran, Safet, and Robert would undergo multiple operations, extensive physical therapy and initial prosthesis fittings. They would slowly begin to realize their loss, their pain, and the uncertainty of their future. They would struggle with whether they would ever be able to go back home. They would also work very hard at improving their English and at learning about American life.

Toward the end of their hospital stay, I took Robert up the hall one afternoon to a pay telephone. He had family and friends in Germany that he wanted very much to try to reach, and I had an international telephone card. He made three phone calls, all very spirited, very joyous, all in his native language, so that I did not understand a word.

We then headed back down the hall toward his hospital room with Robert laboring along on his crutches and dragging behind him the intricate metal contraption that held his leg together. He spoke better English than any of the rest, and he suddenly turned to me and asked, "Are you married?"

"Yes," I said. "My wife is named Nancy."

"Nancy," he repeated. Then he went on, "Do you have children?"

"Yes," I said, "I have two sons, twenty-four and twenty."

"Twenty-four and twenty," his eyes twinkled. "I could be your son!"

I replied very slowly, "Yes, Robert, I know that."

He smiled, understanding the full meaning of what he had said.

Against My Better Judgment

I felt rotten about what I was getting ready to do. But unless I was ready to play God, which I wasn't, I had to sit on my feelings.

Deborah Anne had grown up in my church. She was a sweet, wholesome, slightly naive young woman, very pretty in a southern, home-grown way. She gave you the urge to wrap her in a protective covering to shield her from the outside world. A good heart, a winsome disposition — the community was justly proud of her.

Her family was solid, her father a literature teacher, her mother a doctor — both wonderful people. I could not imagine how they felt about the situation that was developing, but I could not ask. "Parents' worst nightmare," I thought. I felt great sympathy for both of them.

Deborah Anne had brought home Arthur, wanting to marry him. A worthless, disgusting, self-centered beach bum, Arthur turned me off immediately. He went by the name Roddie, which came from *hot rod*. I wasn't sure which reference his friends had in mind, his automobile or something else. He announced his nickname with an emphasis that conveyed that he thought he was the coolest article on the strand and that the strand was the only place in the world that mattered.

He was from Florida, an avid surfer. He worked in a surf shop—what little he worked. He wore a deep tan, the kind you gawked at when you were fourteen because you only saw them once a year at the beach. Later you realized that it was a first-class ticket to skin cancer.

Arthur never looked you in the eye. Doing so would have required that he acknowledge you, demeaning his status. He shifted his attention from side to side, giving the distinct impression that he desired to be through with this conversation as quickly as he could.

The last thing he seemed interested in was serious discussion. He bounced from one flippant comment to another, showing off his cool by spouting sassy one-liners.

"Where do the two of you expect to live?" I asked.

"We'll find somewhere," he replied.

"How will you earn money?"

"There's always money."

"When might you think about having children?"

"Children are beyond my world of interest." His summary comment was, "I just want to get through whatever we have to do here." He was disgusting.

I have been tempted more than once to say to people getting married, "Look at what you're doing! Stop now! It's wrong!" The necessity for this advice, I have learned, correlates not at all with education or intelligence. Some of the most accomplished people I know have proven horrible at picking their own spouses. Some of the most simple have done masterfully. I thought Deborah Anne was making a horrible mistake, but I kept quiet.

She was convinced that Arthur was wonderful. She could not see the narrowness of his little beach world, his nearly total lack of capacity to participate in a meaningful relationship.

Roddie would kick Deborah Anne around for a year or two, let her do all the work and take care of him, accuse her of whatever was wrong, exploit her, and leave her behind for the next available chick. I was appalled.

But I said nothing. They weren't asking for my opinion.

As we approached the marriage date, little episodes happened. In one premarriage session, I asked Arthur, "Tell me who you are. Who is Deborah Anne marrying?"

Arthur replied, "I have not been given the right to ask you that question, and I don't know why you should feel you have the right to ask me." That ended the inquiry. Deborah Anne still sat starry-eyed.

Four of Arthur's friends arrived from Florida to be groomsmen. They were a bit easier to relate to than Arthur, but they all seemed part of a swarthy, playboy brotherhood, wrapped up in their muscles and their surfboards. I doubted that Deborah Anne stood a chance of breaking into the circle.

The worst moment occurred just before the wedding. In preparation for entering the sanctuary, I had lined up groom and groomsmen, all of them dressed in tuxedos. I had signaled to the organist that we were ready whenever he was ready to start the wedding march. I glanced behind me to make sure all the men were lined up in order. As I did, I saw a large bottle of bourbon passing from one mouth to the next, giant last-minute guzzles supposedly designed to calm nerves. The only groomsman omitted was Deborah Anne's thirteen-year-old brother, who looked thoroughly befuddled. I almost stopped the wedding right there.

The couple was married—uneventfully—and left for Florida.

Seven years later, I was greeting worshipers after church one Sunday morning. Before me appeared Deborah Anne, looking a touch more mature but very much the same. "I wanted you to see my girls," she said. Two precious daughters, ages three and five, were holding her hands, peering up at me.

"It looks like I did pretty well," I said.

"You did great!" she replied. "Couldn't be better. These two little things absolutely own their daddy's heart. Arthur works for the convention bureau, arranging big conventions that come to town. He'd be here today except that they have fifteen thousand barbershop singers in town this weekend. I taught school for two years, but now I'm taking care of our girls. We're doing great!"

I stood amazed. Most human beings are in the future what they were in the past. Virtue usually begets virtue; no-good usually produces no-good. A few people, however, turn corners. And I learned once again how rotten I am at predicting which ones.

Deborah Anne and Arthur are still happily married. It would never have happened if I had had my way.

Community at a Crossroads

Henry Triplett grew up in the 1930s and '40s in Owensboro, Kentucky. Having attended college and law school at the University of Louisville, he became a lawyer in

Louisville. Not very many years after that, this very able, very likable young man with the vintage Kentucky southern drawl became a district court judge. In two more decades, he would be selected by the *Louisville Courier-Journal* as one of the three most humorous men in downtown Louisville, a reputation gained from his years of telling hilarious tales and anecdotes from the history of his native region.

Raoul Cunningham grew up in the 1940s and '50s in Louisville's West End, a center of African American culture. In the wake of the U.S. Supreme Court's May 1954 *Brown vs. Board of Education* decision, Louisville quickly adopted a "freedom of choice" student attendance policy in its public schools. All students could enroll in the school of their choice, although transportation was not provided. Raoul, along with a number of other African Americans, chose to travel a modest distance from his West End home to attend Male High School, a few blocks southeast of downtown, traditionally one of the strongest white schools in the district.

Henry Triplett and Raoul Cunningham met for the first time on a morning in March 1961. Henry was on the district court bench. Raoul was the leader of several student demonstrators who had been arrested the previous afternoon for sitting in at the basement lunch counter of Stewart's Dry Goods, Louisville's largest department store.

Henry Triplett described the racial climate in which he grew up:

> When I was growing up in Owensboro, there wasn't a hostile relationship between whites and blacks. It was just whites were here, blacks were there, and that's the way it was. We had one fellow who used to come cook at our house, Columbus Jones. He was also a preacher. Everyone

loved Columbus—maybe for the wrong reasons, but they did. And, I remember Ella. I've never seen anyone since who could fry chicken better. She was a domestic. We paid her five dollars a week, and once a week we'd take her home and take the laundry and she'd do all that for about two bucks. And then there was Smokey, who had the most beautiful Model T automobile I've ever seen. Kept it shined. And he had a real loud voice, and he liked to engage people in conversation, although the other person might be a block away. They were all characters. Everyone loved them. Everyone looked after them. That sort of thing.

Raoul Cunningham has very different memories: "When I was a small child living on Seventh Street, the main shopping district was Fourth Street, which was within walking distance of the house. A lot of times, my mother, grandmother, and I would walk to town. I always wanted to eat and never could. My mother explained it to me: 'We can't.' She had a policy that if she couldn't sit down to eat, she wasn't going to stand to eat. I remember that lecture very well. So, I was aware of it, and I think most blacks growing up in Louisville were aware of it. You could see people eating—you couldn't eat. You could see the movie theaters with the marquee—you couldn't go there."

In Louisville, African Americans as early as 1956 had demonstrated to gain access to downtown stores. In 1958 the downtown drugstores had complied. In 1959, the NAACP had started a major effort to end the entire Jim Crow tradition in downtown Louisville, focusing its attention on a showing of *Porgy and Bess,* with an all-black cast, at the Brown Theater. Little progress had been made. On January 4, 1960, a delegation of thirty-five black and white leaders had gone to City Hall to request an ordinance banning all downtown segregation. The mayor of Louisville had turned them away, announcing that while racial segregation was morally wrong, he could not support a law denying business owners the right to determine who could and who could not patronize their establishments.

In February 1960 students at North Carolina A&T in Greensboro, North Carolina, had begun sitting in at the city's F. W. Woolworth lunch counter. The Greensboro sit-ins had quickly sparked similar student actions in Atlanta and in Nashville.

Through February and March 1960 William W. Beckett, Louisville's lone black alderman, had attempted to get the board of aldermen to pass an open accommodations ordinance. He had failed. The remainder of 1960 had witnessed sporadic demonstrations in Louisville, but no sustained efforts. By the end of 1960, Louisville's black leadership had been in considerable disagreement and conflict over how to proceed.

In this context, in January 1961 a group of teenagers from Male and Central High Schools decided to stop waiting for the adults to do something. With Greensboro, Atlanta, and Nashville fresh in their minds, they prepared themselves and then acted on their own. Their first action came when a small group of them requested service at Stewart's Dry Goods' lower-level café. The manager declared the café closed and locked its doors. This standoff went on for a couple of days. Before the week was out, however, Stewart's stopped closing the café and instead summoned police. The demonstration's leaders, including Raoul Cunningham, were arrested.

The demonstrators have vivid memories of those events. In the words of one of Raoul's friends, Deanna Shobe Tinsley, now an administrator with the Louisville/

216

Jefferson County Public School, "We decided that what we would do is go to the cash register. Eight of us were going to go and one at a time show our money and ask to be served. And that was really our first demonstration. We talked a lot about following the rules that we had read about in the southern demonstrations and the main one was to be calm, to be nonviolent, not to say anything except to be respectful and ask to be served. So we did that."

Raoul said, "We did it on a weekend. We picketed together, and we demonstrated down in the basement of Stewart's, and we closed them. We spread the word around real quick. And we went back. The next day, there was about fifty or seventy-five of us. Each time we went back, it grew. The day that they arrested the first of us, we had targeted Kaufmann's and Stewart's. There were eighteen of us, and we just converged on the stores. Five of us were arrested. They released us to our parents. We had to go to court the next day. Henry Triplett was the judge."

Another student friend, Eleanor Poignard Cockerhan, recalled, "Judge Triplett gave me a stern warning. He said, 'Don't ever let me see you back up here again.' But then he saw me the next day!"

The sit-ins piled up. The arrests piled up. The court cases piled up—according to Judge Triplett's records, there were more than five hundred.

Henry Triplett says now that he did not want to treat the students as delinquents, that they were some of the best young people in Louisville. They had no business being in his court, which had more than enough bona fide lawbreakers to keep it occupied.

He went to Owensboro over a weekend to visit his family. He had an uncle there whose judgment he respected greatly, a conservative old gentleman who had run a business in downtown Owensboro for years. He visited the uncle and described the entire situation in Louisville. The uncle listened carefully. "What should I do?" Henry inquired. "What do you think?"

"Throw the whole thing out of court," the uncle replied. "Those students are not asking for anything they don't deserve."

Judge Triplett did so the following Monday morning. He voided all charges and ordered the police to stop arresting student demonstrators. Of his action, he recalled, "I just thought the juvenile court was the wrong forum for deciding this. I let them all out in one day. The reaction to my decision was mixed, but mostly very favorable. The police were glad to get out of it and not have to lock these kids up once or twice a week. The people who were still singing 'Dixie' before Sunday dinner, they were against it. The other side was totally for it."

The sit-ins continued.

Rallying behind a telegram from Dr. Martin Luther King Jr., stating that "If 50,000 blacks in Montgomery can walk in dignity for a year, surely 75,000 Negroes in Louisville can stop buying in protest for a month," local NAACP and CORE leaders announced an economic boycott of all businesses targeted by the students. That led to the "Nothing New for Easter" campaign, which one of the high school students, Arminta Poignard, described as "like taking ham hocks and collard greens off the table, like taking Christmas off the calendar." The boycott was extremely effective, however, with virtually the entire West End African American community taking part.

Business establishments across downtown Louisville, including Stewart's, began to open their doors.

In March 1962 a newly elected board of aldermen created the Louisville Human Rights Commission to identify
and address community grievances. (In the late 1990s, I
have been honored to serve as chair of that commission.)

Finally, on May 14, 1963, the board of aldermen passed
Louisville's public-accommodations law, declaring that
the doors of all licensed businesses were to be open to
all people regardless or race or color. It was the first such
city ordinance in the South. The high school students
had finally won their cause.

The students now, more than three decades later, make
interesting comments about their participation. Raoul
Cunningham says, "It affected me in several ways.... I
think the commitment aspect may be most important. If
you believe in something, you are going to have to make
a commitment to that cause. That followed me through
Howard [University], and that followed me when I worked
for the Democratic National Committee, and it certainly
followed in a lot of the campaigns I have been involved
in.... I think my commitment to civil rights, my commitment to government, all came from there."

Deanna Tinsley reflects, "It gave me purpose. It really
made meaning of my life during a time when there was
not much meaning. I didn't write. I wasn't crazy about
school. I wasn't a sports person. It was just as if a person
were looking for something in life to latch onto, and I
was lucky. It really was great; it helped me to shape many
of my thoughts. It was a wonderful, wonderful experience. I'm glad I participated. I wish my children had it
so they could have latched onto it, to have a sense of
history, to feel important because maybe they made a
difference somewhere, to feel that early in life."

Recalls Eleanor Poignard Cockerhan, "It gave me a
feeling of power, that I do have the power to effect

change.... I think a large percentage [of people today] think they are powerless.... I know what can happen when people get together and do decide something needs to change. I know it can happen. I saw it happen. I don't think kids today have really seen any effective change going on in their lives. Or the power, the power that comes with knowing that if we stop buying tomorrow, we could bring this country to its knees. Well, see, I know that, [but] I'm not sure the kids today know that.... I don't feel powerless, not at all. I think we can effect change anytime we decide we want to. No, I don't feel powerless *at all!*"

And Judge Henry Triplett says,

> It really caused me to think more and more how wrong this matter of segregation is. Particularly government-sponsored segregation.... More and more I thought it was just totally wrong. One of the big catalysts in my thinking involved the Westwood Presbyterian Church. It's a middle-class black Presbyterian Church. It's got the teachers, the lawyers and doctors, and the public administrators. I met a woman one time in a lawsuit. She was on the other side of the case, and I was taking her deposition. I asked what she did when she was not working, and she said, "I work at my church." I asked her which one. She named that church. And after the deposition, we got to talking, and she said, "We have the best Christmas music of anyplace in the world. I'll send you a written invitation to come to our next concert." So I went down there. Here are all these people dressed up to the nines. And I was listening to the most beautiful music I'd ever heard in my life. I looked at those people and I said, "How utterly and absolutely wrong segregation is."... I think that was a profound thing to happen to me.

In February 1995 the Presbyterian Forum, sponsored monthly by Highland Presbyterian Church in a downtown hotel restaurant, heard Raoul Cunningham describe his involvement in the 1961 student sit-ins. I sat mesmerized through the account. I almost fell off my chair when Raoul said, "The next morning at nine o'clock, we appeared in district court before Judge Henry Triplett." Henry Triplett, one of the members of Highland Church, was sitting a few feet away, smiling. It turned out that he and Raoul had kept up through the years and had become friends. Henry had known full well that he would be part of the story.

I came away from that forum profoundly convinced that we had to conduct oral interviews with the people associated with the 1961 sit-ins, both students and city leaders. I was able to recruit Gwynne Bryant Potts, a Highland Church member and history teacher, and Dr. Tracy K'meyer, the director of the Oral History Center at the University of Louisville, to take part in the project. With their leadership, the event was researched and the interviews performed. We were able to interview five of the students, Judge Triplett, chief of police William Bendner, and several other Louisville leaders. Complete interview tapes and transcripts now reside in the oral history archives at the university. Our work team condensed the interviews into a forty-seven-minute dramatic presentation appropriate for a church sanctuary. It was presented in March 1998 at Highland Church and is to be subsequently presented in other locations. The drama has also been presented twice by drama students at the university.

Quotations included in this story come from the oral interviews.

Henry Triplett was elected to the Louisville board of aldermen in the late 1960s and became a very progressive force in the city's life. He is now a partner in the law firm of Bennett, Bowman, Triplett, and Vittitoe.

After graduating from Howard University, Raoul Cunningham became the chief administrative assistant for Kentucky State Senator Georgia Powers, the first African American woman to be elected to the Kentucky Senate. Senator Powers served for twenty-two years, and Raoul served with her during much of that time. He is now an upper-level administrator with U.S. Corrections.

Conclusion

Retrieving these stories, fashioning them into something presentable, and getting them on paper has been exhilarating. I remake my relationships with the characters; they stand beside me again in living presence. I converse with them about the meaning of what happened: would they have seen what I see or something different? I experience again their courage, their insights, their fears, their blindness. I am aware of how their lives have created my own.

Two things especially I have taken from them. One is the insight that the most sturdy and courageous hearts often come in very plain packaging. It is impossible to tell from the outside who the giants will be. You have to be attentive, to watch and listen carefully, sometimes to dig to uncover the people you really want to meet. High profile is no guarantee of substance. The most interesting people are often well hidden.

The other is the importance of conviction, of having in your soul a motivating cause, a moral purpose beyond yourself for which you are living. It is easy to drift through life rudderless, with no particular direction, simply enjoying the moment and doing whatever comes along. The people I have found myself respecting most are those whose lives are founded on a conviction that transcends them, something worthwhile to which they remain devoted. As they approach the end, they certainly know why they have lived.

The lives of these people of conviction beckon our entire region forward toward a new future, toward a time when all of us can live in the sunshine.